£3

BEYOND
LOGIC
&
MYSTICISM

QUEST BOOKS
are published by
The Theosophical Society in America,
Wheaton, Illinois 60189-0270,
a branch of a world organization
dedicated to the promotion of the unity of
humanity and the encouragement of the study of
religion, philosophy, and science, to the end that
we may better understand ourselves and our place in
the universe. The Society stands for complete
freedom of individual search and belief.
In the Classics Series well-known
theosophical works are made
available in popular editions.
For more information
write or call.
1-708-668-1571

Cover design
by *Anne Kilgore*

BEYOND
LOGIC
&
MYSTICISM

TOM McARTHUR

*This publication is made possible with
the assistance of the Kern Foundation*

The Theosophical Publishing House
Wheaton, Ill. U.S.A.
Madras, India/London, England

Quest
Books

The Theosophical Publishing House
306 West Geneva Road
Wheaton, IL 60187

A publication of the Theosophical Publishing House, a department of the Theosophical Society in America.

Library of Congress Cataloging-in-Publication Data

McArthur, Tom (Thomas Burns)
    [Unitive thinking]
    Beyond logic and mysticism / Tom McArthur. —1st
      U.S. ed. p. cm.
    Originally published in 1988 under title: Unitive
    thinking.
    ISBN 0-8356-0659-7 : $8.95
    1. Thought and thinking. 2. Whole and parts
(Philosophy) 3. Thought and thinking—Problems,
exercises, etc. 4. Whole and parts (Philosophy)—
Problems, exercises, etc. I. Title.
BF441.M36 1990
153—dc20   89-40620
                                    CIP

Printed in the United States of America

The author is grateful to Messrs Thames and Hudson for their concepts of Figures 4 and 7.

Contents

Publisher's note: This work was first published in Great Britain under the title *Unitive Thinking*. British expressions and spellings have been retained.

For Meher, Roshan and Alan,
in whom the twain *did* meet.

Introduction

Unitive thinking isn't new. What *is* new is the prospect that more people can grow into this kind of thinking nowadays than have been able, free, or encouraged to in the past. Seeing things whole has always been something of a rarity, regarded as the secret of élite brotherhoods of mystics or as the special province of poets, prophets and visionaries.

The public response to it over the centuries has been ambivalent. Many societies have swung between reverential awe towards unitive thinkers and the desire to punish, imprison or even kill them for such crimes as heresy and subversion. This is not quite so likely to happen these days, although people can be disturbed by the implications of a way of thinking that alters – undermines? – their everyday assumptions and attitudes. In a world of fractured cultures and global interdependence, however, the practical value of a more comprehensive kind of thought is being increasingly appreciated. It is being seen as both valuable for its own sake and useful in fuelling 'post-industrial society'. It is even appreciated as helpful in getting and keeping an interesting job.

But there *are* risks along the way. For me and for you.

The risk for me is that by packaging the more intellectual side of traditional mysticism I may create yet another bandwagon with a slogan like 'How to win friends and influence people' or 'The power of positive thinking'. That could happen. However, even if it did, 'unitive thinking' does not by its very nature follow fashion; it draws on a wide range of traditions and techniques, and is tough enough to survive being trendy for a time.

The risk for you is dissatisfaction with self, the kind of frustration that the disciples of Japanese Zen masters are expected to feel. They are challenged to re-see and re-think *everything*, which is no small requirement. In the process they realize that there are no instant remedies to the pain and confusion of existence, and no easy short cuts, but that there are intriguing prospects too, as the techniques begin to take hold.

Unitive thinking, and the approach to life that usually goes with it, defies conventional linear presentation. This means that a conventional book – word following word, page following page, chapter following chapter – is not necessarily the best medium for such a subject. I have to use the medium, as it were, to overcome its own limitations. As a result, this typically linear book does not have a typical beginning, middle and end. In an important way every chapter is the same chapter, but approached from a different angle. Any definitions or principles offered aren't absolute recommendations or commands – 'Do this and you will be thinking unitively by next Tuesday'. They are more in the nature of signposts.

There are no certificates in unitive thinking. Indeed, the certificates provided by colleges can often be counter-unitive, as they herd people towards greater and greater specialization, into tighter and tighter boxes of the mind. To be an expert in such a world is to know a lot about a little, and a little about everything else, which is an inefficient procedure in the modern world. We badly need techniques for inclusion, not exclusion. This book is a kind of scaffolding erected for that purpose, to be pulled away when the new inner structure can stand alone. It is a tool that uses language to get at something larger than language, and employs diagrams for what cannot be reduced to diagrams. It is therefore not much good as a 'how-to' book, but fine as a playground for a mind suddenly let out of school.

1

Split Circles

The blurb on the cover of the paperback calls it a 'shocking new superthriller'. It warns that 'an exotic Asian assassin is about to trigger an international explosion of espionage and murder', which indeed she does. She is 'the seductive Sonji, a deadly temptress trained to use the erotic arts to inflict sudden death' – and within the first few pages of the book she uses them gruesomely on a corrupt dictator.

The paperback in question is Steve Shagan's novel *The Circle*. In addition to sporting exotic, erotic assassins, it flirts with both traditional Asian mysticism and the Chinese martial arts, and is not the first thriller in recent years to do so. Flirting with oriental mysticism and martial artistry is fashionable among Western thriller writers these days, as witness Trevanian's *Shibumi* ('Over two million copies sold!' sings its cover) and Eric Van Lustbader's *The Ninja* (whose cover asserts the uniqueness of its 'original action sequences'). Setting aside the superlatives and the sales figures, however, we can focus on the symbol that Shagan chose as central to his story.

It is quite simply a compartmentalized circle. That circle appears on the flag of South Korea, described as follows on the fourth page of the book: 'The cold wind stirred the flag of the republic flying over the modern government buildings, its very design in conflict with the buildings it graced. The red and navy blue circle with its black yin and yang bars represented the essential unity of all being: past and present, good and evil, male and female, life and

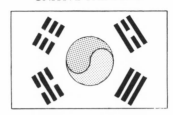

Figure 1. *The flag of the Republic of South Korea. In the flag, red is uppermost in the circle, with blue below, while the black 'Yin' and 'Yang' bars represent the solid male and broken female lines of the I Ching trigrams. A version of the circle from this flag is the cover design of Steve Shagan's novel* The Circle, *with blood dripping heavily down from the red through the blue and out of the circle.*

death – all harmoniously contained within the perfection of the circle.' (See Figure 1.)

The Circle was first published in 1982. Two years later, at the Grosvenor Hotel in London the actor Sean Connery was interviewed by representatives of the magazine *Penthouse,* a publication which also sends out eager signals from the shelves of bookstands. The Scottish actor gained his principal fame, or notoriety, by playing the secret agent James Bond in a series of major movies. In the first of these, Bond's task almost single-handed was to overcome Doctor No, a wily Oriental superscientist not far removed from Fu Manchu. Both of these fictional demons, like Shagan's seductive Sonji, are part of the West's ambivalent response to the inscrutable East, out of which seem to come in almost equal measure both horror and hope.

'Are you interested in oriental religions at all?' the interviewer for *Penthouse* asked the man who was James Bond. This followed an exchange about growing older and just possibly wiser. Connery had mentioned chats with a Muslim friend who valued wisdom, thus prompting the question.

'I've gone through that phase,' said Connery. 'The *I Ching,* playing with that, and Ouspensky's *In Search of the Miraculous,* reading that, and Gurdjieff, and *The Tibetan Book of the Dead.* At the end of the day, the core of these things, it isn't so dissimilar to the Bible. I mean, you throw the coins for the *I Ching* and get the lines, and yin and yang around, and finally arrive at a few commonsensical statements which could apply to almost any circumstances and which you could find in almost any spiritual teaching.'

The *I Ching* is an ancient Chinese work that blends cosmology with both fortune-telling and do-it-yourself psychology. There is no Western equivalent, but if the Gospels had a set of Tarot cards attached to them they might approximate to the style of the Chinese classic. Its underlying assumption is that nature and the human race are not distinct, as many Westerners suppose, but one flowing totality. The patterns of life are expressed by means of composite symbols that are for all the world like a Legoland of universal truths. These symbols, or so the tradition goes, were first discovered over four thousand years ago by the Emperor Fu Hsi while examining the shell of a tortoise.

The basic elements of this psychological Lego are the female cosmic principle Yin and her male partner Yang. In broad terms, Yin and Yang are all the dualities of life such as earth and sky or wet and dry, imagined originally as the shadowy and sunny sides of a hill. Most commonly the symbolism is circular, as in Figure 2, but for the purposes of the *I Ching* there is a more overtly sexual base: a broken bar for Yin that is a stylized vulva, and a solid phallic bar for Yang.

These bars are fundamental in the fortune-telling or self-analysis associated with the book. They can be built up firstly into sets of three (the trigrams displayed in both Figures 1 and 3), and then into sets of six. There are eight trigrams and sixty-four hexagrams, with each hexagram tied to a chapter of the *I Ching*. To do what Sean Connery calls 'yinning and yanging around' one uses three coins and builds up the bars in the fashion described under Figure 3.

Figure 2. *The traditional Chinese Yin–Yang diagram. In such diagrams, the female is red or black and the male is white. The curvilinear border suggests flow and harmony, the 'blendability' of the two principles, while the eye of each tadpole is the seed of one that is always present in the other.*

The outcome is the reading of a chapter of the *I Ching* – and relating its contents to one's current situation in life.

It is not my purpose here to promote the use of the *I Ching* and the Yin–Yang bars as a device either for fortune-telling or self-analysis (although it can be intriguing to try them). Rather, right at the outset of a book about unitive thinking and its symbolism, I want to draw attention to a system used in China for centuries that is entirely outside Western logic – indeed, that is at odds with Western logic. In addition, I also want to demonstrate that for the Chinese themselves the well-known split-circle symbolism of Yin and Yang is only *one* possible symbolism, and that the dualities of life can be shown as successfully (from their point of view) with bars. Symbols are nothing much in themselves, but can mean a great deal when used in particular ways. The more powerful and efficient the symbol the more we can get out of it. In this chapter I am not in fact concerned with what fortune-tellers get out of the *I Ching*, and will say no more about trigrams and hexagrams. I am concerned, however, about what you and I can get out of the split-circle symbolism of Yin and Yang together.

By and large the Western world is far more accustomed to Yin

Trigram	natural image	qualities
☰	heaven	creative, active, strong
☷	earth	receptive, yielding, devoted
☳	thunder	arousing, causing motion
☵	water	deep and dangerous
☶	mountain	still, resting, calm, steady
☴	wind/wood	gentle, enduring, penetrating
☲	fire	clear, light, clinging
☱	lake	joyful

Figure 3. *The eight trigrams of the* I Ching. *Someone using the Yin and Yang bars to consult the* I Ching *starts off with three coins of the same kind. Heads has the value 3 and tails is worth 2. The coins are thrown all together in six successive throws. Following a simple table of values, the total for each throw creates a bar. Starting with the first bar as base, the inquirer stacks six bars successively one on top of the other until a hexagram (or double trigram) is created. This final hexagram has a number and a value equivalent to a chapter in the* I Ching. *That chapter is then read and meditated upon.*

and Yang in their circular form than in the shape of contrasting bars or lines. Most Westerners, whether or not they have an interest in such Eastern systems as Tao or Zen, have never yinned or yanged around, and do not know how to. However, the symbolism of the split circle intrigues many, from artists to scholars of religion. One such scholar, with a considerable interest in Yin and Yang as cosmic symbols, is Geoffrey Parrinder, Emeritus Professor of Comparative Religion at the University of London, who describes the concept in some detail in *Sex and the World's Religions*, published in 1980.

In the preface to this work Professor Parrinder warns potential readers that the book is intended neither for 'those who regard sexual intercourse as sinful' nor for 'the salacious, looking for saucy titbits' – as they might do in *Penthouse*. His study is a straightforward and fairly neutral work of scholarship whose aim is 'to see others as they have related sex and religion to each other, and thereby to see ourselves better'.

It is clear from this introductory remark that the book, though worldwide in its coverage and eclectic in its style, is not intended for a worldwide audience as such. Its 'ourselves' apparently refers to the Western – and essentially the Christian – world, while the 'others' to be studied are in the main Eastern. Despite the seeming distance between them, therefore, Steve Shagan and Geoffrey Parrinder have a shared interest: what the Orient is and does. The East of course reciprocates the interest, but with a marked predilection for the material and technological goodies that the West offers.

In his study, Parrinder notes that 'the duality of the sexes is one of the oldest and most usual ways of representing universal powers and relationships'. In China, the traditional cluster of meanings and associations for the complementary dualities is:

YIN	YANG
female	male
passive	active
dark	light
weak	strong
receptive	penetrating
vaginal	phallic
Earth	Heaven or Sky

Parrinder contrasts these basic Chinese symbols with an equally well-known bit of dualism from farther west: the warring Persian gods of light and darkness. Only one of these, either Ahura Mazda or Ahriman, can win the final battle for the universe. However, where their opposition one to the other is total (and totally male), Yin and Yang are not fundamentally opposed at all (and are both male and female). Indeed, as Figure 2 shows, there is a seed of Yin in Yang, and a seed of Yang in Yin. Few theologians in the Western religions that still operate the Persian opposition would admit to a seed of Satan in God or a touch of God in Satan.

Let's put the God/Satan opposition side by side with the Yin/Yang harmony. The first of these gives us a Persian or 'Western' option that is essentially *divisive* and adversarial; it proposes that never the twain shall meet, except as enemies. This is *either/or* country. The second, however, the Chinese or 'Eastern' option, is essentially *cohesive* and conciliatory – and this is *both/and* country.

These make two options for handling all the pairs of opposites

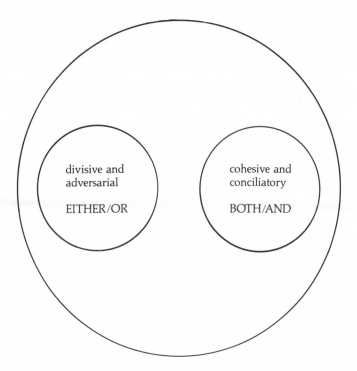

divisive and
adversarial

EITHER/OR

cohesive and
conciliatory

BOTH/AND

in the world. There is, however, a third and *unitive* option, which as it were puts both the Western and Eastern options inside a larger circle still (see the diagram).

You get this effect by rising above or distancing yourself from the first two options. Call it 'transcending' them if you wish, or think of it as more elbow room, and a refusal to be limited by one vision of how things are. At this level of understanding one has, as it were, *two* visions. One can (at the very least) choose to go the way of division and *either/or*, or go the way of cohesion with *both/and*. Let's try this out in a simplified way with an everyday concept rather than with the metaphysics of Tao in China and Zoroaster in Persia. Take a simple split-circle diagram with the word SUCCESS on one side, as in the second diagram. We are virtually impelled to fill the empty half with the word *failure*; you could almost say that the word appears of its own accord – of necessity – in the empty space. With these antonyms we can first of all apply the *either/or* option, asserting that the world is divided into two kinds of people, those who succeed and those who fail. Doing this, we write off certain people as failures in life, or cop out by proposing that some people succeed because they are 'naturally' successful people. This is rather similar to saying that God and goodness are always in one half of any circle, and the Devil and evil always in the other half. The second option of *both/and* offers broader scope. It implies that success and failure interrelate: there are those who sometimes succeed and sometimes fail, who succeed in some things and fail in others, or whose success turns into failure or whose failure turns into success.

Unitive thinking, however, allows for both options or for either

of them *in permanent suspension*. One need not be limited either divisively or cohesively. Public examinations, for example, are generally pure *either/or*: the wheat on one side and the chaff on the other. Human relations are often pure *both/and*, as for example when people say: 'I don't want to judge; there's good and bad on both sides.' And the grey areas abound, even in something as apparently clear-cut as war; it is not always easy to distinguish the victors from the vanquished.

All of which may seem self-evident, but it is by no means self-evident for all things on all occasions. Try it with God and the Devil – or with heterosexual and homosexual. That is when the third or unitive option can turn into social dynamite, because it is entirely unyielding in what it throws up.

Rudyard Kipling, in his poem *If*, talks about meeting with Triumph and Disaster and treating those two 'impostors' just the same. That is an important element in the unitive option, because creating the great circle that contains the lesser options requires that height and distance which together constitute detachment. With the right degree of detachment one can make thoughtful assessments of polarities like success/failure, God/Satan, heterosexual/homosexual, and the like.

The Hindu mystical poem the *Bhagavad-Gita* looked at matters like these some two thousand years or more ago. In it, the hero-god Krishna offers advice on the eve of battle to his dispirited friend, Prince Arjuna. Part of that advice is to treat gold and dirt as just the same. Arjuna, like the rest of us, finds that advice hard to accept, because gold and dirt are so patently not the same. But apply the three options in order. Option 1 keeps them permanently apart, the one lustrous and rich, and other dull and worthless. Option 2 enlarges the picture by linking them in their common mineral origin, perhaps pointing out that seeds can grow in dirt but not in gold. Moreover, gold-dust has often been referred to as 'pay-dirt'. Option 3 allows for the others as needed, and you are not forced into either mould. You can step back to take a better look at what is going on. In the process, you might also see that the circles aren't really split at all. The split is in our minds and in our languages, and in any case the circles are simply symbols, not ultimate truth.

The split-circle idea is actually built into the structure of this chapter. Rather than simply start straight away with the business of options, I opted myself for a Yin of the sexy superthriller followed by the Yang of scholarly dispassion. Steve Shagan with his vivid novel and Sean Connery talking to the representative of a girlie magazine occupy one half of the circle, while Geoffrey Parrinder warning his readers about both asceticism and salaciousness (plus my own discourse on options) occupies the other half.

Apply the three options here. Option 1 keeps the worlds of Shagan and Parrinder for ever apart – a world of glitz and hype opposed to a world of academic objectivity. Option 2, however, allows them to meet and flow together; everybody on earth can take an interest in *I Ching* hexagrams and Yin–Yang symbolism, for their variegated purposes. Option 3 accepts that in certain circumstances there is a gulf fixed between *Penthouse* and the works of Emeritus Professors, while in other circumstances bloody Yin–Yang diagrams will appear on the covers of sudden-death superthrillers. And finally, the gold of one and the dirt of the other have an impostor quality about them anyway – and each of us must decide which is the gold and which the dirt, and in which measures. Whatever else happens, the use of the three options helps us perceive and then re-perceive the possibilities *in every set of opposites under the sun*.

The Yin–Yang device proposes to us that the universe is a seamless robe, and also that in everyday life we cut up this uncut robe into all sorts of shapes and patterns, the most basic of which is a straight (or a curved) cut down the middle. Woman is then distinct from man and sky distinct from earth, and a word like *success* distinct from a word like *failure*. And so they are for many purposes, and so they are not for many other purposes. In addition, a circle is also a wheel, and wheels can turn. The Hindus have a tradition of the wheel of life and death, in which everything and everybody turns, taking on fresh shapes, only to dissolve and reshape again and again.

The Yin–Yang circle can be used like that. Or, to follow the theme of gambling as we saw it in the *I Ching* diagrams, we can see the circle as a roulette wheel – or even as the face of a clock. Suppose, as people often do, that the hands of a clock only go one way; that is, they only have one option open to them. Option 2, however, supposes that they can run both ways, and in fact we do talk every day about 'counter-' or 'anti-clockwise' movement. With a picture like that in mind, one can manage the flow of success into failure and failure into success in interesting and effective ways, because there is no reason to suppose that a direction like this is irreversible. An attitude that allows for reversal of direction can change one's whole conception of triumph and disaster. The seeds of future success can be present in present failure – and, unfortunately, vice versa. Option 3 is a constant reminder of this. On its level of observation there is no such thing as just one option. Both options are always there, in a state of dynamic tension that you are free to enjoy or dislike, or both, or something else.

The more options one has, the greater the power to cope. It is like choice in a supermarket as opposed to choice in the corner store, however convenient and friendly the corner store. Better, it is like choice in the supermarket *and* the corner store.

Follow-up to Chapter 1

● The following short story is from a Unitarian course on human relations. What are its Yin–Yang implications?

> A father and son were travelling by car on an outing that took them across a railway level-crossing. Alas, the car stalled on the crossing and, despite desperate efforts, the ignition key stuck and the car refused to move before a train came and smashed into the car. The father was killed instantly but the boy was rushed to hospital and prepared for an emergency operation. But on entering the theatre, the surgeon took one look at the boy on the table and said, 'I cannot perform this operation. That boy is my son.'

● Imagine that you are an Irish immigrant fleeing the potato famine of the mid-nineteenth century and taking ship to America, the Land of the Free, or a Jewish refugee from pogroms in Poland catching sight of the Statue of Liberty. Then imagine that you are an African slave on a cotton plantation before the Civil War, or a Sioux Indian watching white gold-seekers pouring into the Black Hills of Dakota. Build a split circle for the United States out of these pictures.

● The novelist Robert Louis Stevenson published *The Strange Case of Dr Jekyll and Mr Hyde* in 1886. Writing about its centenary in the magazine *English Today*, Barbara Brill notes in July 1986: 'Stevenson himself took to using Jekyll and Hyde in letters to his friends and relations, as a code name for good and evil striving for ascendancy . . . in April 1886 when Stevenson had taken his elderly and mentally-sick father on holiday he wrote home to his mother: "My father, I am sorry to say, gave me a good dose of Hyde this morning." ' Create the split-circle options for such 'split personality'.

● A *koan*, says the *American Heritage Dictionary* of 1985, is 'a riddle in the form of a paradox used in Zen Buddhism as an aid to meditation and a means of gaining intuitive knowledge'. It is, in effect, a technique for unitive thinking. Below is a classic Japanese koan. What are its Yin–Yang implications?

What is the clap of one hand?

● Put each of the following words, one at a time, into the left-hand side of a split circle, as I did with SUCCESS. What happens?

WAR	YOUNG
BEAUTY	NEW
LOVE	BRIGHT

● Could the Star of David symbol be said to have anything in common with the Chinese Yin–Yang circle?

2

Pregnant Triangles

Some three thousand years ago the legendary Hindu sage Yajnavalkya called each human being 'a half-fragment', and was probably the first person to put forward the theory of the soul-mate.

The theory is simple enough. In the beginning there was one living soul, of the size and shape of a man and woman tightly embraced. That being divided, said Yajnavalkya, becoming on one side the first man and on the other side the first woman, who then reunited in conscious sexuality and begat the human race. There was a kind of incestuous quality to it, and to escape from this the woman fled into the shape of a cow. But the man became a bull, and from their union all cattle have come. She then became a mare, but he pursued her as a stallion, and from that union all horses have come. So they continued as pairs, until everything that lives and moves in the world came into existence.

But it is still part of all such creatures to yearn for unity again, said the sage, and in seeking for it through sexual coupling they both continue their races and prolong their nostalgia into further generations.

There is a particular esoteric tradition in India that calls itself 'the loom', an English translation of the word *Tantra*. On the warp and woof of Tantra all the webs and patterns of life are woven, including one of the greatest love stories in the world. This is the cosmic romance of Shiva and Shakti, which goes through cycles of asceticism and eroticism to match the mood-swings of Hindu culture. In 1946 the German Indologist Heinrich Zimmer wrote about it, pointing out that the symbolism of Shiva and Shakti – like that of Yin and Yang – is just one of many ways in which the unity of existence splits up into 'antagonistic yet co-operative pairs of opposites'.

The cosmic love-story of Shiva and Shakti is a red-blooded affair. In it Shiva loses his soul-mate time and time again, but always finds her and unites with her again. On one occasion when they rediscover one another it is to give life straight away to a hero who will save the world from the ravages of an otherwise invulnerable demon. Although both god and goddess can be ascetic yogis they can also be passionately sexual, a statement of the dynamic tensions of life but in a Hindu form that is far more immediate and human than the refined abstraction of Yin and Yang.

Figure 4. *The Primal Pair, so tightly embraced that they are unaware of their separateness. While they are united in this way, the world exists. When they part, the world dissolves.*

In Figure 4 the primal couple are in deep embrace. In Tantric theory the universe is safe as long as the embrace continues, but when the partners draw apart it begins to dissolve. When Shiva and Shakti are separate, there is no universe, but when need for each other brings them into their next union the universe blossoms again, and is sustained through its next cycle.

However, as commonly as the Divine Pair are represented as human lovers they are depicted as triangles. An upward-pointing triangle is Shiva as the male cosmic principle, while a downward-pointing triangle is Shakti as the female cosmic principle. When the triangles are apart there is no universe; when they touch, tip to tip, it is either about to blossom or about to vanish; and when they are enmeshed the universe is vigorous (represented in Figure 5 as the Star Hexagon, more commonly known in the West as the Star of David). When that star begins to revolve it becomes the wheel of life and death with all its options and possibilities. The

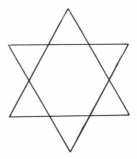

Figure 5. *The Star Hexagon, the blended male and female principles, a geometric version of Figure 4.*

major difference, however, between the Hindu Shiva–Shakti and the Chinese Yin–Yang is that for the Hindus the female is the active principle and the male passive, an intriguing reversal of the Chinese view.

In Tantric tradition magical diagrams called *yantras* are commonplace. Also sometimes known as *mandalas*, these devices are seen as a means of focusing the mind in meditation. They serve as what the Indologist Georg Feurerstein has called 'cosmograms' – maps of reality comparable to the *I Ching* diagrams. One such yantra is known as the Shri Chakra or Shri Yantra, translated either as 'the wheel of fortune' or as 'the supreme yantra'. It is a complex design, made up of a square enclosing a wheel enclosing sets of meshed triangles (Figure 6), and is a detailed depiction of what happens when Shiva and Shakti are entwined.

The outermost element of the yantra, the square with its gates for the four directions, stands for the physical world. The circle immediately within it is the cosmic lotus, the totality of life, within which in turn are the triangles that are proof of Shiva's and Shakti's fertility: the pairs of humans, cattle, horses and so forth that have devolved from the one that is two and becomes many. The triangles combine and multiply in the frame of the yantra just as the Yin–Yang bars combine and multiply in the frame of the *I Ching*, its hexagrams, and its sixty-four chapters.

Westerners who pride themselves on a no-nonsense pragmatism and a commitment to logic have no difficulty dismissing such diagrams as oriental fripperies on a par with astrological charts and the reading of tea-leaves. That is a pity, because this curious magical geometry serves both to reveal and conceal, as it were,

Figure 6. *The Shri Yantra or 'Wheel of Fortune', a Tantric device depicting how all forms and pairs emerge from the coming together of the primal pair.*

a whole way of viewing existence. Philip Rawson has westernized it in his *Tantra: The Cult of Ecstasy*, published in 1973. In this book he says that the Tantric view of time is the reverse of the ordinary, everyday view. In the ordinary view, we are like people sitting in the back seat of a car who are only able to see out through the rear window. Such a condition is like Figure 7, which is rectangular this time: the frame for everything we know. Inside that frame, the Tantric triangles have been converted into rectangles too. These represent objects that 'appear out of an invisible future' and become observable through our rear-window view of things, framed in the present moment (which defines our immediate sense-experience and knowledge):

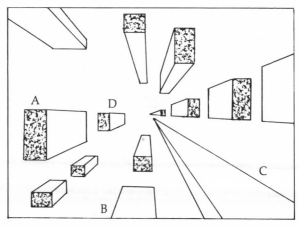

Figure 7. *The everyday view of life and time, as if seen through the rear window of a moving vehicle.*

'As time goes by things, as they get older, seem to recede towards the horizon. All things seem as though they must have beginnings and ends. A is a person we have known all our lives who has died. We can "see" his life entire from beginning to end. Other people and things, like B, have begun and are still with us. Some existed, like D, far back in history. Others, like the earth, at C, may *seem* to have been always there. But our astronomy suggests that in this kind of time the world may have had an infinitely remote beginning, at the central vanishing point of our view of all things . . .

'But of course, if the frame actually represents any person's sense-experience at a present moment, he cannot really have experienced what the objects even a small way back from him towards the horizon were really like. He has to "make them up" as mental fictions, helped out by "scientific knowledge". We don't any of us really "know", from our own direct experience, what every moment of even quite recent history was like, or the lives of our friends, or even whether things are there that we don't experience. In addition, we easily forget that we ourselves, as bodies, should each be one of those receding boxes, and that each of us has his own frame of the present which is being formed into a box of its own, which to people looking out through their own frames of the present will look like A. For when we are dead that is how we will look to someone else.'

Rawson may use rectangles instead of traditional triangles, but his view is none the less 'standard' Tantra. It presents existence as a marvellous game-like illusion, the product of our minds and senses as they cross-check through all our experiences and memories of experiences. Given such a model of receding reality, we exist in the present and try with the help of that model to prepare for the future. Thus, we may be able to predict and be ready for Rectangle E when it enters the frame of the present – or it may come unbargained for, and hit us like a brick.

Tantra says: Well, yes, this is a convenient way of looking at things, but it is not the only way. Suppose, for example, one reversed the whole conventional process, turning as it were in our seats to look ahead *over the driver's shoulder*?

If we were to do that, we would see into the very face of creation. Since this could be terrifying, Tantrics have tended to depict this forward-looking vision as a monster's face, out of whose mouth spew all the shapes of existence, including you and me. Rawson updates this ancient image by comparing the Mouth of Time to the blazing exhaust of a rocket, which is a dream-like shift in the metaphor of the vehicle. Another Tantric image of raw creation is even more basic: a womb or vagina-mouth endlessly spilling out new shapes. The traditional Hindu name for all of this is *Maya*, which is represented as an active and seductive female force whose name is both 'creativity' and 'illusion'. Another name is *Lila*, which means 'play', and the two are occasionally combined as *Lilamaya*, which is the play of creative illusion, the unending bursting bubbles of fiction that we perceive as facts.

All of the geometric devices that I have so far used are convenient fictions. In themselves they have no ultimate worth, any more than the line of the equator or the face of a clock has ultimate worth. It is how we employ them that matters. As unitive devices they can be best understood in terms of two master devices: the container and the continuum.

I have already called the universe a seamless robe. This image is not far removed from the Tantric metaphor of a loom or the common Hindu metaphor of Maya as a web woven around us that also includes us. A continuum as such is not a robe, a loom, or a web, however, but we are unlikely to be able to grasp its nature unless we use such metaphors. If I turn to the world of liquids, I could say that a continuum is something that flows in all directions. Water can be a good image for a continuum, and water in a bottle is a very good image of a continuum bounded and shaped by its container. If such a bottle, full of water, were put in a bath full of water we would get an image close to many used in classical Hinduism. The bottle would be you or me, individuals with apparent shape, a shape which helps us forget that what is inside the container is the same as what is outside it. Smash the bottle, and the two waters become one (again), the small continuum joining the larger. Similarly, when we cut up the seamless robe of the universe it remains uncut, whatever we suppose we are doing. The cuts and containers are there, certainly, but in a fuller sense they are not there at all.

In language, there is no end to what we might say, but the moment we say something the continuum is 'containerized' into specific words, each with its bottle-like shape and its 'content' of meaning. Taken together, the words we produce are little containers all strung together, all of them receding into the past as in Rawson's Rectangle. Once said, the container-words cannot be called back again, but they also have the quality – Lego-like – of being available again and again in new combinations for new message-strings.

People think of languages as containers. 'French' is the language used by 'the French' in 'France', and 'English' is the language used by 'the English' in 'England', as if the languages were coterminous with certain container-states. But they are not; their continuums spread out to the Swiss and the Belgians, or to the Scots, the Irish, the Welsh, the Americans, the Australians, and so forth – and even inside countries like 'France' and 'England' the languages are not uniform: there are varieties galore, for which 'dialect' container-names may be necessary.

Crude container models are useful, as useful as, say, the Option 1 of the split-circle diagram. Sometimes, however, it is necessary to complement the Yin of container modelling with the Yang of continuum modelling. When we are straightforwardly contrasting languages like French and English, for example, we can accept that they are distinct entities, but we must also accept that over the centuries great quantities of French have flowed into English, and that French today is by no means impervious to English – whatever certain French politicians may feel, defensively, ought to be the case. The idea that there is a French-in-English and an English-in-French brings both the container and the continuum model fruitfully together, and allows us to see that a supposedly distinct language may well contain much of another language.

Like languages, the subjects that we study and talk about are not neat containers either. Try putting – and keeping – a subject like 'politics' in a box labelled POLITICS, and keeping other subjects like 'religion' and 'economics' out of the politics box. You will fail, because all such containers leak into each other, just as all our ideas and experiences leak into each other. Suppose you were born into a family of convinced capitalists. Suppose also that in later life you encountered someone who was born into a family of convinced communists, for whom capitalism – your greatest treasure – was a crime against the human race. You could choose to regard the Marxist as an alien and an enemy, or at best as a specimen for thoughtful analysis (and rejection). Your opponent, of course, would be entirely free – if that is the right word – to do the same. You could then fight a war to see who would win and inherit the earth. This kind of thing of course has happened a lot in the past, whether or not the labels and ideologies were at the time 'capitalism' and 'communism'.

If, however, you applied the basic model of the split circle, you could increase your options before going to war. You could assume that you occupied one half of the circle and the Marxist the other half, and that the halves of the circle could be either closed or open to each other. You could talk, if of course you could persuade your opponent to join you, like Reagan and Gorbachev in Geneva in 1985. If you genuinely saw capitalism and communism as halves of a circle called 'economics and politics', then you might for a diversion try Option 2 and think of them as complements, each saying something useful about the nature of economic and other relationships, and *that* could have an interesting effect on your whole outlook. You could very well, in the process, cease to be a whole-hearted *laissez-faire* capitalist and your opponent might cease to be a dogmatic and convinced communist. Simply the effort to understand one's opponent sincerely would have that effect. (You could also, of course, both become 'traitors'.)

Suppose, though, that we pushed the model a bit further, from the circle with its one continuum and two containers to the Tantric world of one continuum and an infinity of possible containers (more being constantly provided out of the Mouth of Time). Using this more generous model, we would see that there are far more options on the continuum of politics and economics than the capitalist extreme and the communist extreme. All kinds of benchmarks are available to us along this line, allowing for conservatives, centrists, liberals, social democrats, democratic socialists and so forth, and if we spread the continuum a bit further we could add in fascists and anarchists, utopian socialists and Christian Democrats, not to mention pro-life anti-abortionists, Green-party ecologists and others who do not see why politics and economics should be restricted to boxes labelled 'politics' and 'economics'.

When I was eighteen I found myself in a difficult and thoroughly divisive situation. At the time I was a student at the University of Glasgow in Scotland. The city of Glasgow was also my home town, with a population about evenly split between the Yin of Roman Catholicism and the Yang of Protestantism. Until I went to the university I had never met a Catholic socially, and had not been aware of the lack. But people from every community in the city sent daughters and sons up to Gilmorehill, and this Protestant son met somebody else's Catholic daughter. Combining Shakespeare with a modern medical buzzword, you could call this the Romeo-and-Juliet Syndrome, and sit back to watch the sparks fly. They did. Our families were as upset as the Capulets and Montagues, and I found to my surprise and deep distaste that my 'normal' upbringing had – without my ever thinking about it – built a hate reflex into me that even romance could not override.

I disliked the reflex so much that I set out to get rid of it, and not just because of our on-again, off-again romance. One of the methods I used in a summertime of travel was to call in as a hiker at Pluscarden Priory in Morayshire, where I had heard they welcomed visitors. The Benedictines certainly welcomed *me*. I stayed with them for most of a week, had my own small room, ate with the monks in the refectory, and attended their services as and when and if I liked. I also had free access to their library, which had been bequeathed to these Anglican-turned-Catholic monks by a local Presbyterian minister. And, above all, the Prior invited his small group of guests for conversation in his study after the evening meal, and that conversation roamed off in all kinds of directions.

In my second year at the university I enrolled for Moral Philosophy, a dryish subject into which religion was not supposed to leak. My tutor, however, proved to be a Catholic and was intrigued when he learned in our general chat that I had spent some time during the summer at Pluscarden. He lent me a book by Bede Griffiths, a former Prior there. I enjoyed the book and said so when I returned it, and was offered a follow-up book that also had far more to do with heaven than Hobbes. At that point I realized my tutor reckoned me ripe for conversion, which was embarrassing, because I wasn't, and felt it necessary to clear the air by pointing this out. Our relationship was never the same afterwards. When I handed in my next essay – on the required class-wide subject, 'Is Morality Natural?' – I received a low mark, accompanied by the written comment from my tutor: 'Don't bring religion into an essay on Moral Philosophy.'

I felt violated, firstly because he had brought it in, and secondly because I saw no reason why it could not be brought in – and was glad when that particular term and tutorship ended. If I had told her about the incident, my cousin Isa would have said, 'Well, what else can you expect from a Romanist?' Alas, in the world of Glasgow's Catholics and Protestants my tutor had played his stereotypical role all too well. But in the world of Pluscarden Priory and my on-again, off-again romance, the stereotypes could not survive. *They* enabled me to break out of the half-circle – the ideological container – of my prejudice.

The apocryphal tale is told of some bully-boys in Northern Ireland who got a stranger up against a wall, demanding to know whether he was a Protestant or a Catholic.

'I'm neither,' he managed. 'I'm a Jew!'

'Aye, but are you a Protestant Jew or a Catholic Jew?'

When you want containers badly enough, you'll stuff everything in the world into them, to get the right shapes.

Follow-up to Chapter 2

● At the beginning of the chapter I credited the Hindu sage Yajnavalkya with originating the idea of the soul-mate. The classical Greeks discussed this idea too. In Plato's *Symposium*, for example, there is a tongue-in-cheek account of how all human beings were once 'hermaphrodites' (that is, unions of the god Hermes and the goddess Aphrodite). Zeus split each of these conjoined creatures in half, since when we have been born with a feeling of loss. Biology now demonstrates that when two human 'halves' come together, they each provide a half-cell (a *gamete* or 'marrier'). The half-cells combine into a *zygote* or 'yoked one', creating in effect a tiny hermaphroditic gift. What does this say about 'mythology' and 'science'? Or about human beings?

● Philip Rawson draws a picture of past time, receding from us. If past time is a road stretching behind us, a corridor or a lengthening line, what symbol might best represent the present? Think about what happens as you think about this.

● *Tao*, says the *Longman Dictionary of the English Language* (1984), is 'the principle of creative harmony' and 'the path of virtuous conduct' as described by ancient Chinese sages. The book called the *Tao Te Ching* says:

> Tao begets One; one begets two; two begets three; three begets all things. All things are backed by the Shade (yin) and faced by the Light (yang), and harmonized by the immaterial Breath (ch'i).'

Is this what the driver of the car sees? Have you ever had – or how often do you have – the feeling that everything is really just one? How many of your closer friends have had a feeling like this? Have you ever asked them, or would you be willing to ask them now?

● There is a Zen statement in the classic *Hsin-Hsin-Ming* which has some bearing on the tutorial incident in my Moral Philosophy class at Glasgow University. It runs: 'If you want to get hold of what it looks like, don't be against or for anything.'

● Imagine a prisoner in a cell. Then imagine the cell door swinging open. What happens next? Why?

● In your general routine, do you always go somewhere on a certain night of the week, and are you upset when such a routine is disturbed? Do you tend to get up and go to bed at the same times every day? Do you always know the date and the time, or do you sometimes forget what day it is? Are you governed by time-tables, or are they a convenience to make *your* existence easier? Are you bothered by these questions, or are they just questions?

3

Frames and Fables

Let us suppose, for the sake of discussion, that in the year 2000 a vessel comes out of deep space from the region of the star Arcturus. We can also suppose that it identifies ours as the only planet in our solar system with life on it, and that to study that life it goes into orbit round the earth.

The crew of this starship are not at all like us. They call themselves *kluuls,* and when they talk they hiss, whistle and chirp rather than cutting up sound with lip, tongue and teeth as we do. They are also a cautious folk, in no hurry at all to make personal contact with any Earthlings. They therefore set up a visibility barrier round their vessel just to play safe, and settle down for one complete *haalhh* – a major unit of their time – to analyse us. Using their extremely efficient bioprobes they have little trouble in cracking the codes of our media, our computers, our languages and – in passing – our genes.

Kluuls of course are saurians and born out of eggs. They are therefore intensely curious about females with wombs and live births. Before they turned the domesticated *thóofkh* into a bio-computer their way of recording data was to write on their own sloughed-off skins, discarded as they passed from one maturation phase to the next. They are therefore also intrigued by our inability to do this, and by a terrestrial writing system that depends on sheets of dried-out mashed-up plant fibre. But more than anything else it is our system for measuring and arranging time that catches their interest. It is truly unparalleled in all the worlds from Betelgeuse to Rigel.

Some of the system makes immediate sense, of course. A human 'year', for example, is comparable to a kluul haalhh, because each is the time needed for the home planet to get round its sun. But where a haalhh subdivides into five because of the five great algae harvests, the twelve human subdivisions of the year derive not from something so obviously useful but from the wanderings of the single natural satellite that orbits Earth. In addition – and this causes a few scales to ripple – both the tides of the Earth's seas and the rhythms of the human females' fertility are also tied to the comings and goings of this 'moon'.

The human concept 'day' is also graspable – initially at least. It relates to the rotation of the planet on its axis, in relation to the light of the planet's single sun. But the kluuls find themselves at a loss to understand how this unit 'day' can be both the complete period of rotation and the part of that rotation set against 'night'. As a result, 'night' is both a part of 'day' and the opposite of 'day'.

In addition, they were at first at ease with the base number twelve for time-units like months, hours, minutes and seconds – then encountered the unit called a 'week'. They were still mulling this seven-day anomaly over when one researcher announced that the major calendar of the Earthlings ran in two directions at once – a forward direction called 'AD' and a much larger backward direction called 'BC'. This, the kluuls decided, must mean that Earthlings identified only with a minute part of their species' history, a conclusion which made them glad they had put up their visibility barrier. Such beings must be seriously disturbed.

The kluuls from Arcturus are not the only creatures who have puzzled over the units of time that we so casually take for granted. In 1985, an American professor of sociology wrote a book about the week: *The Seven Day Circle*, by Eviatar Zerubavel of the University of New York at Stonybrook. A whole book of 206 pages . . . One reviewer, Lisanne Renner of the *Orlando Sentinel*, was so intrigued that she telephoned the professor for a personal quote, which ran:

> 'Here there is a social order that is purely arbitrary, yet it looks as if it is natural. You have an endless river of time and you create seven-day structures to give order to it, and I find that mind-boggling.'

Mind-boggling, and not just interesting. In this Zerubavel is different from most people, who may never have done more about the week than growl when Monday arrives and welcome the onset of the 'weekend'. The unitive quality in Zerubavel is his unwillingness to take the thoroughly familiar for granted. Sheer familiarity has a sedating effect; by dulling the edges of our sensibilities it lets us get on with all sorts of other, less fixed, less predictable matters. Given a conventional frame like a week or a year, we can use it as a setting within which to organize both our activities and ourselves. The turning year even provides us with an anchor-point, the repetition of that day on which we were born, so that we can calculate precisely where we are on the lengthening thread of our lives.

To inquire about the frame seems eccentric. To question it disturbs a deep neatness. It is the peculiar mark of small children that once they have learned such things they do not take kindly to having them tampered with, but paradoxically it is also the case that when our frames *are* seriously wrenched out of shape small children can adjust better to the changes than many adults. In this, for survival purposes, they have a unitive flexibility behind the façade of their junior conservatism.

There is also a price to pay for the convenience of the familiar, and most people pay it without a moment's thought. When the edge of sensibility is dulled the edge of wonder can be dulled with it, the kind of wonder that allows Zerubavel to call the week 'mind-boggling'. Few people inquire about the etymology of Wednesday or the curious circumstance of the Monday-morning feeling or the Friday-afternoon car in the assembly plant. They pay more attention to Sagittarius than to November, because the frame of the Zodiac – like the *I Ching* diagrams – is more exotic than the frame of the everyday year. And it offers more scope for fantasy and fortune-telling.

Zerubavel's metaphor of 'an endless river of time' is not far removed from my metaphor of existence as 'a seamless robe'. He discusses structures for dividing up this river, while I have been talking about cutting up the robe of life with, I suppose, the scissors of the mind. As regards time and its measurement, some of the divisions have been pre-arranged by nature, and cannot be changed: the distance of earth from sun, the presence of one moon behaving in predictable ways, the speed and angle of the planet's rotation on its axis. Others of the divisions have, however, been dealt to us in a cultural card game and *can* be changed (although changing them may cause howls of disapproval).

We are, for example, in the 'twentieth' century only because our Chirstocentric calendar says so, and for the time being has triumphed over alternative calendars. If we had still been using in Europe the Roman calendar then the present year would be about 2740 AUC, where 'AUC' stood for *ab urbe condita*, 'from the founding of the city'. In our own calendar's reckoning Rome was founded in minus time, in 753 BC.

The week, however, *is* mind-boggling. Zerubavel traces its origins to two ancient sources that coalesced: the seven days of creation in the Hebrew story that we now call 'The Book of Genesis', and the seven heavenly bodies of ancient Babylonian astrology-cum-astronomy (the old divinities now having a mix of Roman and Teutonic names in English). Among the Hebrews *one* day was set aside as the Sabbath, the Lord's Day, which Christians, however, shifted from the Jewish Saturday to a somewhat pagan 'Day of the Sun'. The Muslims in their turn in due course chose Friday as their pivotal day of prayer. Zerubavel calls this kind of shifting 'calendrical contrast'. If rivals want to be different from each other, what better way than using time differently? Meanwhile, many modern cultures continue to experience end-of-week creep, as the idea of *two* or two-and-a-half days of 'weekend' leisure takes hold more and more firmly.

However, despite all this evidence that the week is a cultural creation, scientists who call themselves 'chronobiologists' have found that it also has a natural element. They have identified week-like rhythms in plants and insects that have never counted the heavenly bodies or been taken to church on Sunday. Lisanne Renner reports that in human beings blood pressure and hormones have cycles of around seven days, and 'human kidney, heart and pancreas transplants are most likely to be rejected at seven-day intervals'. Franz Halberg of the Chronobiology Laboratories of the University of Minnesota coined the expression 'circadian rhythm' for the cycle of around 24 hours that operates on all of us for certain purposes. To this he has recently added 'circaseptan rhythm' for the seven-day cycle that appears to have been dealt to us in the evolutionary card-game.

Thus, the week is the point where the *natural* measures of time (sun and year; moon and month; rotation and day) meet the *cultural* measures (seconds, minutes, hours, decades, centuries and millennia, together with our minus/plus calendar), because it operates in both spheres. And if some people hadn't begun asking questions about the obvious and familiar, we would not now know that. The deadly *So what*? reflex did not apply for them, nor the cautionary observation that 'if God had wanted us to fly he would have given us wings'.

The best traditional unitive symbol for the kind of openmindedness that I am talking about here is the headstand in physical yoga. Quite regardless of what it may do to and for the internal organs (see Figure 8), the primary characteristic of *sirshasana* is that it inverts. There is a concise and appealing reminder of this in Robin White's novel, *Men and Angels* (1961), set in southern

Figure 8. *The Yogic Headstand. The headstand or sirshasana is for many people a defining symbol of yoga. Practitioners of yoga extol it, when it is properly done, as a means of reversing the effects of gravity on the body – freshening the blood supply to the head and neck while relieving the lower body and legs. It is said to prevent wrinkles and to promote youthfulness, encouraging the ability to concentrate and meditate. It should, however, be undertaken under adequate supervision and with great care, so as not to harm the spinal column and the blood vessels of the head. People with disorders of blood pressure should not rush into it without proper medical counselling.*

In addition to their capacity, properly handled, to promote physical and mental well-being, the yogasanas *or stylized poses of yoga are symbolic In sirshasana, by going against gravity one physically prepares for going against the familiar, the accepted and the conceptually safe. This can also require a degree of caution.*

India. Luke and Sarojini have come to consult the learned scholar Professor Mahalingam, and find him standing on his head. When the professor sees them on the veranda he calls them in and starts their conversation without himself coming out of his inverted pose. Luke, the ever-amazed American, asks him what he is doing.

'Relaxing,' the professor says. 'It is my custom both at sunrise and sunset. The gravitational forces on the body become inverted, you see, and so also the conventional manner of looking at things, thus freeing the mind from blocks to clear thinking and relaxing the nervous system. I find it good for digestion as well.'

The yogic symbolism of the headstand is not far away from the English expression 'to stand something on its head', meaning to look at it or treat it from a completely different angle. I have already touched on the idea of reversal, where I suggested that both the split circle and the blended triangles can be visualized as rotating, and therefore capable of running in both directions. The headstand is comparable. The stylized rotation, inversion, or reversal of anything – a person, an object, an idea, a symbol, a point of view – through 180 degrees is usually informative. It is also close to the Tantric idea of turning right round and looking over the shoulder of the driver rather than always out of the rear window of the car.

Just as the idea of Yin and Yang was built into the structure of the first chapter, so the idea of reversal is built into the arrangement of this chapter. In the first instance, I approached an earthly matter – the measurement of time – from the oddest angle I could think of, a starship full of kluuls from Arcturus. I took their hatching from eggs and tradition of writing on their sloughed-off skins as an outrageous 'norm' against which to assess human biology and traditions. There are venerable precedents for this kluul's-eye view: the classic fables of Aesop, Plato's Simile of the Cave, Lilliput in *Gulliver's Travels*, as well as the marvellously informative works about Alice by Lewis Carroll. It is interesting that such books are often disguised as children's stories or relegated to the shelves of children's fiction. It is a measure of how people handle materials couched in unitive form. Who, one wonders, are the children?

Crudely, for present purposes, let us suppose that all the 'poses we adopt and the frames of reference we erect are in principle invertable. An immediate benefit is disturbing the familiar, and an intriguing by-product can be those occasions when societies kick over the traces of everyday convention and have a festival where everything is upside-down. Clowns become kings and kings become clowns. The Roman festival called the Saturnalia was just such an occasion, and in the Western world Saturday is still the day of the week when the work ethic is for many people temporarily set aside. It can also be splendidly ego-deflating to come at one's most precious obsessions and demands from a wholly different angle, even something as basic as, 'Who'll be worrying about this a hundred years from now, or even a hundred days?'

Suppose that a conclave of chronobiologists and other experts on time-systems got together under the auspices of the United Nations. Suppose that they then discussed for a year and a day the shortcomings – temporal, cultural, religious and ethnic – of the AD/BC calendar and came up with a wholly new conception for a global system. They look for the dawn-time of civilization, and find it in the approximate date of the founding of Eridu in Mesopotamia, the world's first ever city. Suppose they then propose that the year 2000 when it comes will be 5500 AE ('After Eridu'). Then, in a fit of unanimity, the nations of the world agreed to adopt this calendar from AD 2000 onward. What would the consequences be like – first of all inside your own head, then for you and your friends, then for the world at large? Would it be worth doing? How would people feel about it two hundred years later, in 5700 AE? Has there been anything at all comparable that has happened in your lifetime, anything that so thoroughly changed the frame?

The Yin–Yang and Shiva–Shakti symbols are readily recognizable as frames, as indeed are the chapters I introduced them in, as is this book itself. It may, however, take a little longer to perceive systems like, say, Protestantism of one kind or another, Roman Catholicism, the Republican or the Conservative Party, and so forth, as framing devices too. The kluuls of course would see this instantly, from their virginal perspective, but it is a lot harder for us who are in or near the frames themselves. To get at what I mean, though, I would like to leave our present time-frame and go back to ancient Egypt.

The Egypt of the Pharaohs was by and large the first ever unitary state, and Egypt since those days has gone through many metamorphoses, without, however, breaking its remarkable thread of continuity. Nowadays, when people talk about 'Egyptian mythology' they are not thinking of anything recent. Most present-day Egyptians would probably assert that mythology in Egypt came to an end long ago. It means Isis and Osiris and stuff like that, not Coptic Christianity and Islam, which are religions with Books, and therefore conceived as mirrors of truth. What the ancient Egyptians believed in might be interesting, but it was not *truth* of the same calibre at all. 'Paganism' is the commonest word for such things as gods with animal heads and mummified cats.

We know what we mean by a phrase like 'Egyptian mythology', and normally do not need to meditate on whether it is a rigid container of an idea or a fluid continuum. Let it be both, just like 'Aztec mythology' which blends with 'Aztec religion', and ultimately with 'Greek mythology' and 'Polynesian religion', and so forth. We know this in a general sort of way, and know also that we need these easy compartments of life, otherwise we couldn't talk about anything. All of which is true, but . . .

In ancient Egypt there was a consensus that the world began in a primeval ooze called Nun, out of which emerged a single muddy hill. After that, however, there was no consensus. The priests of Heliopolis, where the sun-god was supreme, told one story of what happened next, and it redounded to the greater glory of the sun. The priests of Hermopolis and of Memphis and of Thebes, however, told other stories, which all demonstrated how a deity dear to them was in at the creation. In Hermopolis, for example, they spoke of how the celestial goose laid an egg on the oozy hill and the sun-bird Ra emerged from that. Hermopolis was a centre of pilgrimage, and one of the relics on view there was the fragmented shell of the great egg laid by the celestial goose.

Nobody cares now about the Great Egg Shell of Hermopolis. Few people have ever even heard of it. But some people who might smile and shrug at such absurdities may be carrying in their pockets air tickets to Lourdes for a cure, or to Mecca for a once-in-a-lifetime pilgrimage that would give them the title 'Haji' – or may quietly hope to have their bodies cremated when they die, on a burning ghat above the Ganges in the sacred city of Benares. Or they might intend some day to file past the tomb of Lenin in Moscow, or visit the Lincoln Memorial in Washington, DC. Or just take the kids to Disneyland, where the celestial bird is a duck.

Such actual and potential pilgrims exist in their millions. In the eye of eternity they are all visitors to the Great Egg Shell of Hermopolis.

Traditionally, mysticism has proposed a kind of double vision, and the principle of invertability is a valued aid in acquiring that peculiar skill. In Indian philosophy one kind of vision looks at Maya, the flux of the world, while the other kind looks at Brahman, the stillness beyond and behind (and yet somehow also *in*) that flux. Brahman is the seamless robe, or the endless river, while Maya is the patchwork into which we turn the seamless robe, or the dams and weirs that we build across the river, marking off its sections.

A 'day', therefore, is a quirk of Maya, where a particular planet happens to rotate in a particular way while it orbits a particular sun/star. An 'hour' is also a quirk of Maya, created from the circumstances of particular cultures. Go far enough away from the culture and there are no more 60-minute hours; go far enough away from the planet and there are no more 24-hour days. Maya melts into Brahman, or so the argument goes. Why not, ask the sages of the Upanishads, recognize this state of affairs here and now, and apply that recognition in your life? It turns everything on its head for a time, but – who knows? – it might also be good for your digestion.

Follow-up to Chapter 3

● The dog is often called 'man's best friend'. Man has occasionally been called a god for dogs. What is a dog's-eye view of people really like? *Or* a bird's-eye view?

● Here is another *koan*. How does it fit into the idea of reversal or inversion?

Where does my fist go when I open my hand?

● Try these news items:

○ Headline: OPPOSITION LEADS IN USSR POLLS.
○ The Archbishop of Canterbury, the Most Reverend Judith Rosenthal, officiated at the ceremony.
○ The 13th Commonwealth Games in 1986 were subject to a series of political misfortunes.

● Here is an excerpt from Lewis Carroll's poem *The Hunting of the Snark*. How does it relate to Maya and Brahman?

He had bought a large map representing the sea,
   Without the least vestige of land:
And the crew were much pleased when they found it to be
   A map they could all understand.

'What's the good of Mercator's North Poles and Equators,
   Tropics, Zones, and Meridian Lines?'
So the bellman would cry: and the crew would reply,
   They are merely conventional signs!

'Other maps are such shapes, with their islands and capes!
   But we've got our brave Captain to thank'
(So the crew would protest) 'that he's bought us the best –
   A perfect and absolute blank!'

● You may or may not be a seasoned world traveller. Whether or not you are, imagine yourself first of all in a country where they speak the same language as you (say, the UK and US, or Spain and Cuba, or Sweden and Denmark – more or less). Then get on a plane in that country to another where the language is quite different but the signs are in the same script (say Turkey or Finland). Then travel on to a place where both language and signs are different (like Saudi Arabia or Japan, if you are a Westerner). In this last country leave everything except some local money in your hotel: passport, watch, portable radio, newspapers and books, the lot. Let your interpreter go as well, when you leave the hotel. Get on a train or a bus or a bullock cart and ride to a corner of the land that has been little touched by the world you are used to. Then burn your return tickets. How do you feel as night falls?

● The Kingdom of Heaven, so the New Testament says, is like a mustard seed. Is it?

4

Parabolas

Catherine Devillers is both a translator and an artist, and lives in Quebec. On one occasion we were talking about that favourite Quebec topic, language, as well as about the general problems that people have in communicating with each other – just getting their points across successfully in *any* language.

Catherine duly took up her pencil and began to draw some members of two very distinct societies: the Cubes and the Globes, speakers of Cube Language and Globe Language. No Cube could speak Globe Language, or vice versa, so that on the rare occasions when they met they needed an interpreter. That was the pencil's job, and it was good at it, moving back and forward in this instance between an emissary from each society.

In their conversation, the pencil informed the attentive emissary from Globeland that sometimes the Cube suffered rather badly from corner-ache. When it had heard this, the sympathetic Globe asked the pencil to suggest that Cube and Globe might go for a roll together; that was bound to ease the discomfort. Although a roll, of course, proved out of the question, the two ambassadors parted company amicably enough, each reporting back in due course to their national headquarters. And each of them said to their superiors that, quite clearly and despite appearances, the underlying thought of the two nations was the same. With the Cubes, however, it was assumed that the underlying thought of the Globes was cuboid, while in Globeland it was supposed that the underlying thought of the Cubes was globular.

All of which is a cautionary tale for those politicians, philosophers and linguists who tend to make easy assumptions that the rest of the world is – or must 'really' be – just like us. What the Cubes and the Globes had in common was geometry, but not angles and curves.

Catherine Devillers' cartoon strip, however, is more than just a powerful little cautionary tale. It is a unitive tool, one of the oldest and most effective of such tools in the world. A common name for it is 'parable', a word that like so many other terms of European

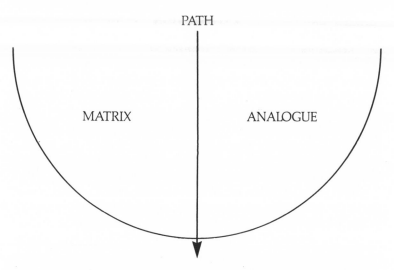

Figure 9. *Parable–Parabola. Imagine the vertical 'focus' line of the parabola as a path from top to bottom. On the left of the path as we see it is the everyday* matrix *of the world, while on the right as we see it is an* analogue *world from which comparisons can be drawn. The point where the focus line and the curve of the parabola meet is the point where the familiar and the analogical come together.*

Years ago, when the clock was an exciting innovation, people needed a suitable word for the presentational circle of the clock. Somebody must have said, 'It's just like a face', pulling the word face *across from the analogue side of the line. Parabolic invention can have odd effects, however. We also needed a name for the pointers that move on the 'face' of the clock. 'They're like hands,' someone evidently said – and so now we have 'hands' in the 'face' of a clock, unlike any creature that ever was. Now, however, no one thinks about how bizarrely the two metaphors fit together. It is all too familiar for that.*

culture derives from ancient Greece. Among other things the verb *parabállein* means 'to set side by side', 'to throw or to turn sideways or obliquely', 'to get near' and 'to compare'. The parabola of geometry also derives from it, a curve of great symmetry that is identical on either side of a line called its focus (Figure 9). Both parable and parabola share the adjective 'parabolic', which describes the delicate obliqueness of both story and shape. Both truth and nature, it suggests, may need to be approached indirectly. Pitchers like Jesus and Socrates were experts at throwing a curve ball.

'A sower went out to sow,' says the Gospel according to Matthew. 'And as he sowed, some seed fell along the footpath; and the birds came and ate it up. Some seed fell on rocky ground, where it had little soil, and it sprouted quickly because it had no depth of earth; but when the sun rose the young corn was scorched, and as it had no root it withered away. Some seed fell among thistles; and the thistles shot up, and choked the corn. And some of the seed fell into good soil, where it bore fruit, yielding a hundredfold or, it might be, sixtyfold or thirtyfold. If you have ears, then hear.'

This is a typical parable, now distributed so widely around the world as to be part of the story-stock of the whole race. It is part of the formula of the Gospels, however, that after Jesus has told such a tale and invited those with ears to hear it (as it should be heard), his disciples receive a decoding explanation (which can leave one with the impression that they were sometimes a bit slow in the uptake). In this instance, Jesus explains the parable of the sower in detail, making in literary terms the following set of correspondences:

seeds on the footpath	the devil comes and leads the hearer of the truth astray
seeds on rocky ground	the hearer is impressed, but the impression does not last, especially in the face of opposition
seeds among thistles	the hearer is diverted and over-powered by the things of the world, and cannot pay proper attention to the message
seeds upon good soil	the hearer has understood and passes on his understanding to others who also understand

Nor does the parable stop at comparing seeds and believers in
Christ. It allows for a third jump *beyond* Christianity to all
situations where messages are on offer, scattered among the public
at large. In our own time, George Orwell has created a comparably
powerful tale in his parabolic *Animal Farm*. Here, the double jump
from parabolic context to first oblique reference then on most
compellingly to a second and more general oblique reference is quite
stark:

Napoleon Pig	Lenin/Stalin	any revolutionary tyrant
Snowball	Trotsky	any displaced revolutionary idealist
Major	Karl Marx	any prophet of revolution
Mr Jones the Farmer	Tsar Nicholas	any fallen *ancien régime*
the Pigs	the communists	any revolutionary party that comes to power; any self-serving clique or élite
the Dogs	the Soviet secret police	any secret police or system of covert surveillance and overt punishment of the un-cooperative
the Farm	Russia or the Soviet Union	any country experiencing a major revolution; any revolutionary situation
Boxer the horse	the workers who have been duped	any good-hearted soul taken in by the revolutionaries

The parable belongs in a family that also includes analogy,
metaphor, simile, allegory and model-making. All such means of
effecting a comparison depend for their effect on a kind of intimate
twinning, a splicing between contexts on the basis of an actual or
assumed resemblance. Thus, if I am talking about people and refer
to the cream of society, I take the single word 'cream' from the alien
context of dairy produce and splice it into my discussion about
human beings, and just as cream rises to the top so certain people
can be found at the 'top' of human society. Similarly, if I refer to

someone seeing the light, I have gone to the alien environment of suns, stars, fires and lamps and have brought back the idea of such illumination into the immediate context of discussion and understanding. Orwell uses a whole farmyard of animals to make his political point, demanding of his readers that they share with him at least a double if not a *triple* vision of what goes on when people revolt. The double vision is the two sides of the focus line in a parabola. Triple vision is a bonus, achieved by expanding the symbolism beyond its initial point of reference.

When we talk about parables and metaphors we enter the wonderful world of 'as if'. Reading the New Testament, the *Bhagavad-Gita* or Orwell's *Animal Farm* we begin to accept double vision as a normal state of affairs. You can also meet it in a theatre, where you can be simultaneously aware of the reality of the stage and seating and the fascination of the play being performed. There is a comparable situation with novels and with films and television. The human race has been engaged in this kind of double vision for a long time; much of art, literature and indeed religion arises out of it. Its primary quality is the creation of a gap between 'reality' and 'let's-pretend', a gap that may well turn out to be more helpful than straightforward literalism.

Sometimes it is impossible to be literal and make any kind of progress. This must have been so when scholars wanted a word for what they studied, and lifted from the vocabulary of farming the word 'field', as in a 'field of learning' and a 'magnetic field' in physics. Time and etymological change can dull metaphoric effects, but triple vision can be found in the word 'current'. In Latin it originally meant 'running' (what animals and people do), then it was applied to what streams and rivers do, then was re-applied to what electricity does, when the flow of electricity was compared, *not* to people running, but to water flowing. So literalized have such usages become – and there are thousands of them – that we take them to be entirely normal, worthy *and dull*. Whereas, with a twist in our perceptions, they can leap into life again and become mind-boggling, just like Zerubavel's seven-day week.

The parabolic style is at its best when a mind is in fresh confrontation with a new problem. It challenges people to 'see' in ways that they have never seen before. Cubes in Globeland have both metaphoric power and a great deal of charm, while kluuls from Arcturus invisibly orbiting our Earth acquire, for a time at least, a peculiar 'life' that is as potent as fact. As Carl Gustav Jung might have put it, they are 'psychologically real'. On a larger scale this psychological reality operates across whole cultures and religions. The compilers of the *Bhagavad-Gita* were no doubt aware of this when they used the imagery of the god Krishna, and inserted their didactic tale into the body of Hinduism's vastest epic, the *Mahabharata*. They knew that millions would receive their story as simple God's-Truth, and treated it as God's-Truth themselves, however elegantly they may have edited it into its present shape. Their parable says: 'Let's see life as a battlefield. Let's imagine opposing armies drawn up and ready to fight, and put a chariot between them. In the chariot there is a driver called Krishna, who knows what is what, and behind him the bowman Arjuna, who has his duty to do but is confused and upset. But you, reader, are really Arjuna – as is every human being who has ever lived or ever will be – and Krishna has something to say to you. So listen.'

Those who have ears, let them hear . . . This instruction applies not just in the sphere of prophets and seers, either, but in everyday life. That is effectively what a master says to his apprentice, when he says 'No, no, no – don't do it like that, do it like *this* – and listen while I explain it again.' It is what cartographers have said: 'Let's pretend there's a line right round the mid-point of the planet and call it the Equator, because there is an equal amount of land on either side.' Or what economists do: 'Let's make a working model of the economy of Finland.'

One of the greatest parables of all time appears in Plato's *Republic*. Plato had an inclination towards the ideal and the mystical and more than any other thinker is responsible for spreading the word and concept 'idea' round the world. The idea in this particular parable was that the human race is like people kept prisoner in a cave, and the story he relates about them is suspiciously like the plight of various unitive thinkers in the past. In fact, in the *Republic*, the story is recounted by his master Socrates, who may well have originated the Simile of the Cave. If that is so, it is richly ironic, because Socrates was himself compelled to drink poison, his punishment for supposedly corrupting the youth of Athens.

'Imagine', said Socrates, 'all these people chained in this cave, with their backs to whatever meagre light filters down from the surface of the earth. Since childhood they have been shackled so that they can look only one way, towards the smooth cave wall farthest from the surface. Behind them is not just the stony path out of the cave, but also a kind of wall where puppeteers can hold up all sorts of things, moving them around and making them dance and wriggle. Up on a ledge behind the unseen puppeteers is a bright fire, and that fire casts the shadows of the puppets and other shapes on the wall in front of the prisoners, who are fascinated by what they see.

'Suppose', he went on, 'that these prisoners were able to talk among themselves. They would talk about the shadows, wouldn't they? They would name them and argue about them, and would believe they were real. They would become quite passionately involved with them, wouldn't they? But suppose that one of these prisoners is deliberately unshackled, then prodded and pushed, made to stand and to turn round, right round, to look first at the puppeteers, then at the fire, then – as he became accustomed to what he saw – at the stony passage through which filtered down another kind of light. [See Figure 10.]

'He would be confused at first, wouldn't he, and maybe irritated and frightened? But he would be intrigued too. Let's assume that he began to explore, and that persuasion or curiosity took him into the stony passageway upward. That would be quite an experience, wouldn't it? Because when he reached the light of day he would be blinded, and would need plenty of time to calm himself and to begin to see. It would be a fearful revelation, of course, because the real sun and moon and all the world would be so different – so much more intense – than the world of shadows in the cave.

'But we should suppose now that the time came to go back – back into the cave and to his old seat and chains. When that happened, of course, he would be blinded again, wouldn't he? But this time the blindness would be due to passing from light to darkness, not from darkness to light. And when at length he sat again among his friends, stunned and shaken, what would he think of them, and what would they think of him?'

What indeed? Plato's own conclusion is relentless, depicting the mockery and laughter as the returnee struggled to adjust his vision once again to the dimness of that place of confinement. They shouted that he had only managed to damage his own eyesight by going off wherever he had gone, and said they would kill anybody who believed his crazy stories.

Figure 10. *Plato's Cave.*

Plato's prisoners all face one way in their cave. Only one is made to turn right round and look the other way. In this, the Simile of the Cave is remarkably like the Tantric view as presented by Philip Rawson, where we stop looking through the rearward window and turn to see what the driver of the car sees. The Platonic simile also deals in two kinds of light – firelight and daylight – which brings us back yet again to the idea of a double vision. We can extend the metaphor in various ways ourselves, supposing for example that kluuls from Arcturus live in one cave while humans on Earth live in another. Or conclude in the end that we all live in separate caves of the mind.

Many belief systems, some very old indeed, have argued just such a case. The Jains of India, the Manichees of Iran, the Albigenses of medieval France and various other sects and cults have insisted that we are spirits trapped in flesh, creatures of light condemned to live in darkness. There are touches of beliefs like these in corners of the great world religions too, among people who deplore the world, the flesh and the devil and dream of higher states where the soul floats free. It has also been common in various schools of mysticism to speak about 'the inner light' or a 'Cosmic Consciousness' in terms of which this everyday world of Maya is dark and dismal. All of them seem close to Plato's Simile of the Cave.

However, if we put the two kinds of light into a split-circle diagram and apply the unitive options the situation may become a little clearer. You can either have the light of this world, flickering and shadowy, or the transcendent light of the other world; or you can have both. Or, Option 3, you can leave your options open. Stripped of the symbolism of the various creeds, the higher light cannot be turned into a higher 'physical' world as such. If we believe that, we misunderstand entirely the analogical basis of the whole story. The higher awareness relates not to a place but to a state of mind, one in which the seamless robe is recognized as the background to the everyday. That unity lies beyond words and beyond visions, and cannot be reached even by the most nimble of metaphors. All such descriptions are like asymptotic lines on a graph. They may approach the horizontal line but they never reach it. They halve the distance every moment, but they never arrive at their goal.

Towards the end of his life, the medieval saint, Thomas Aquinas, expressed the conundrum of existence quietly and vividly. He had spent years in the writing of tome upon tome about theology. His aim was both to reconcile the Christian faith with the logic of Aristotle, Plato's pupil, and to establish the absolute rightness of Mother Church over the arguments of Jew and Muslim. Today, as a result, he is still revered by many Catholics as the great exponent of theological orthodoxy. But in December 1273 he suspended his work on the *Summa theologica*, never to take it up again. He had had a mystical experience, as it is commonly described, while saying mass, and afterwards told his secretary: 'All I have written seems to me like so much straw compared with what I have seen.'

That is a salutary thought for all writers, and can also be a provocative thought for anyone who labours to promote any ideology. *Webster's Ninth Collegiate Dictionary* in 1984 offered four related senses as the meaning of the word 'ideology'. The first and core sense was 'visionary theorizing', followed by the outcome of that theorizing, 'a systematic body of concepts, especially about human life and culture'. That was the kind of thing Aquinas devoted his life to discussing, in a way that reflects the third Websterian sense: 'a manner or the content of thinking characteristic of an individual, group or culture' (especially where an individual like Plato or Aquinas can help shape the thinking of a group or culture). Fourth come 'the integrated assertions, theories, and aims that constitute a sociopolitical program', which often contains plans for preaching the ideology to the heathen and the unconverted, because in the view of the ideologues who have embraced it theirs is the truth, the whole truth, and nothing but the truth.

The priests of Hermopolis once believed they possessed just that, and a token of it in the fragments of the Great Egg Shell. You and I know others with similar convictions, as convinced today as the Hermopolitans were convinced in *their* day, which lasted for a very long time indeed. Priests, ministers, philosophers, gurus and commissars often say 'God is Like This', or 'Truth is Just So', or 'History is Ours'. But there is no hard evidence that God, Truth, or History has been placed exclusively in the care of one human group with one human vision, whatever the claims made for it. That is a thought-provoking statement: for human beings betray a curious willingness, now as in the past, to die for such parabolas of belief, or to put others into uniform to die for them, or to burn others at the stake for not accepting them – shouting, in effect,

'My analogue is better than your analogue!'

Great works of scripture and literature of enduring value lie behind many such systems. The Vedas, the Bible and the Quran, the epics of Homer, Vyasa and Firdausi, the plays of Shakespeare and Molière, the works of Goethe, Tolstoy and Dickens – all these and others in various ways help people define themselves and their societies. Their 'psychological truths' are profound, but too literal an approach to their metaphors of reality, too material an interpretation of their pictures may convert those profundities into slogans for war and into prison cells for innumerable minds.

A great religious, political, or national ideology is a kind of world epic, world drama, or world novel in which each believer is a performer. Some shout in the crowd scenes or have moments of glory in a bit part, but some others are lucky enough to get dressed up and perform for a time centre-stage. All of them, however, have their glory enhanced by the abstractions in whose service they are more than willing to shout, sing, dance, preach, lecture, conform, march and maybe even kill or be killed. Usually we are born into them, sometimes we have adopted them (through conversion or naturalization), and sometimes we can perform in more than one at a time. American Jews and the American Irish can participate, if they wish, in both the religious-cum-national epics of Israel and Eire, as well as in the Saga of the American Dream.

Such ideological tapestries can be glorious or gory, uplifting or degrading, ancient or recent – or a mix of these and more. They are both the best of the human inheritance and the worst of motivations, depending on how we ourselves use them. We need them, tribal forces that give us a psychological shape and direction to match our physical forms and needs. But to use one last analogy here, a touch of unitive detachment can be handy: each ideology may claim to be the Standard Language, but it is far more likely that we are all just speaking different dialects of Truth.

Follow-up to Chapter 4

● Once-fresh metaphors often fade. They can, however, be revived by looking at them from a different angle. Below are colour words on the left and other words on the right. Match them up and think about them. The first is done as a guide.

1	white	a ( )	lining
2	black (*twice*)	b ( )	herring
3	golden	c ( )	list
4	silver	d (1)	lie
5	red	e ( )	moon (once in a . . .)
6	green (*twice*)	f ( )	streak
7	blue	g ( )	is beautiful
8	yellow	h ( )	fingers or thumb
		i ( )	opportunity
		j ( )	with envy

● Try these reminders of the power of metaphor.

Francis Thompson, *The Hound of Heaven*:

'I fled Him, down the nights and down the days;
I fled him, down the arches of the years;
I fled Him, down the labyrinthine ways
Of my own mind . . .'

Edward Fitzgerald, *The Rubaiyat of Omar Khayyam*:

'Awake! For Morning in the Bowl of Night
Has flung the Stone that puts the Stars to Flight:
And lo! The Hunter of the East has caught
The Sultan's Turret in a Noose of Light.'

E.M. Forster, *A Passage to India*:

'Making sudden changes of gear, the heat accelerated its advance after
Mrs Moore's departure until existence had to be endured and crime
punished with the thermometer at a hundred and twelve. Electric fans
hummed and spat, water splashed on screens, ice clinked, and outside
these defences, between a greyish sky and a yellowish earth, clouds
of dust moved hesitatingly.'

S.E. Rasmussen, *Experiencing Architecture*:

'The architect remains anonymously in the background. Here again
he resembles the theatrical producer. His drawings are not an end in
themselves, a work of art, but simply a set of instructions, an aid to
the craftsmen who construct his buildings. He delivers a number of
completely impersonal plan drawings and typewritten specifications.

They must be so unequivocal that there will be no doubt about the construction. He composes the music which others will play.'

● 'My analogue is better than your analogue!' Substitute each of the following words for 'analogue' in this stance, slogan or war-cry, and consider your response each time.

COUNTRY   ACCENT
TEAM   EDUCATION
FAITH   FLAG
CLUB   RELIGION
PARTY   MIND

● Baha'u'llah, the founder of the Baha'i Faith, was steeped in the traditions and symbolism of the Sufis, for whom the ultimate is 'the Beloved'. Here is a verse from his *Hidden Words*:

'O man of two visions! Close one eye and open the other. Close one to the world and all that is therein, and open the other to the hallowed beauty of the Beloved.'

● Imagine human twins on a horse that is standing on a crocodile. Where might one find imagery like that?

5

Compartments of the Brain

In talking about time I referred to a curious usage of the English language: that a 'day' can be *both* a twenty-four-hour period that contains one night *and also* half of that twenty-four-hour period where the other half is night. There are plenty of odd quirks like this in natural languages, and artificial languages like Esperanto have been invented so as to do away with some of them. Usually, however, they do not make great headway, as people are as stubborn about their mother tongues as they are about the ideological systems into which they have been born.

Another curious usage in English relates to what is inside one's head. If people admire the intellectual qualities in a person, they might say, 'She's got a good brain.' At the same time, however, when urging somebody to think harder, they might well say, 'Come on, use your brains – what do you think you've got them for?'

What then do we have inside our skulls – a brain or brains? The language lives happily with both singular and plural, and recent scientific studies seem to back it up. There is a sense in which we do have one cerebral mass, one brain, but there is also a sense in which we have multiplicity inside our heads – *many* more than one brain. The story of these recent adventures in neurophysiology is as bizarre as any I know, and might best begin with the work of two American neurologists, James W. Papez and Paul D. MacLean.

MacLean's work at the Laboratory for Brain Evolution and Behavior at the National Institute for Mental Health, near

Washington, DC, built upon the pioneering efforts of Papez to demonstrate that what we think of as one organ is in fact a kind of layer cake, an evolutionary outcome that is now widely known in physiological circles as 'the triune brain', an organ that is literally, physically and chemically three in one. In the words of Charles Hampden-Turner (in his *Maps of the Mind*, 1981), these three layers, states, or sub-brains are 'distinct in their structure and chemistry, which is revealed by the Golgi method of staining brain tissues. While the functions that they perform are duplicative and overlap, they differ markedly in style.'

In the lowermost position in your head and in mine, around the area commonly known as 'the brain stem', is an ancient neural mechanism that humans share with reptiles. It is, says Hampden-Turner, 'hardly touched by evolution, and found in prehistoric reptiles as well as in turtles, alligators and lizards today'. Surrounding this area of reptilian brain is an outer and higher layer, making up what is commonly known as 'the limbic system', and this we share with such mammals as rats, rabbits, cats, kangaroos, cattle and donkeys. Above and around this old mammalian brain is in its turn our massive new mammalian brain or cerebral cortex, which we share with cats and chimpanzees except that our cerebral cortex (often referred to as 'the neocortex') is very much larger than that of any other higher animal. Commenting on this remarkable ensemble, MacLean observed: 'We might imagine that when a psychiatrist bids the patient to lie on the couch, he is asking him to stretch out alongside a horse and a crocodile.' (See Figure 11.)

Taken together, the two lower crocodile and horse brains contrast

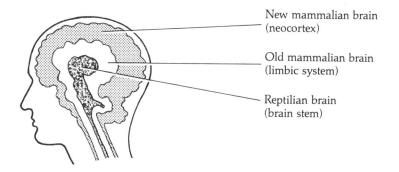

New mammalian brain (neocortex)

Old mammalian brain (limbic system)

Reptilian brain (brain stem)

Figure 11. *The triune brain.*

strongly – as one might suspect – with the higher, more human, brain. The links between the lower organs are considerable: thick neural connections serve them. They consequently work well together, almost as if crocodile and horse were one, the product of millions of years of evolutionary development. These parts of the human system run the basic programs of life: dominance and submission, ganging up on the alien and the weak, defending territory, engaging in sexuality (including courtship and display), and in such related matters as hunting, hoarding, nesting, bonding, herding together and engaging in social behaviour like play and ritual. In sum, they are frames for physical and social survival. Tamper with them at your peril.

Hampden-Turner adds: 'If the limbic cortex is irritated by epilepsy, rabies infection, or experimentally stimulated, sudden gusts of rage, panic, pleasure or "Eureka!" sensations can sweep over the organism, which may snarl, salivate, attack, or become addicted to pleasurable self-stimulation. Such areas seem almost exclusive to the older brains, which also mediate the autonomic nervous system, the body's involuntary internal responses.'

Paul MacLean was, however, disturbed when it became clear to him that, where the two lower brains were strongly bound together, there was nothing comparable between them and the third, higher and newer 'human' brain. The neural links between the neocortex and the crocodile-cum-horse below are delicate and rare by comparison with the links that bind *them* together. It is as though just over half a million years ago – in a biological spasm during the Pleistocene Age – the third brain outgrew the very possibility of such a strong link. Even as long a time as that was nowhere near long enough to build up a strong connection between, as it were, Dr Jekyll and Mr Hyde. MacLean, along with other commentators such as Arthur Koestler and Robert Ardrey, concluded that our species suffers from a 'design flaw'. Says Ardrey in *The Social Contract* (1970), 'The new brain speaks in a language that the old brain does not understand.'

Stevenson's Jekyll and Hyde are not the only images that spring to mind when one considers the bizarre nature of this cerebral composite. Inevitably, imagery from myth, religion, literature and psychoanalysis all crowd in: Beauty is above and the Beast below, God and the angels are above and Satan with all his legions are below – or indeed, in a most provocative parallel, Sigmund Freud's

Super-ego is high above, his Ego is in the middle, and his Id hides in the murky depths. The three levels of the psyche that he mapped out bear an almost uncanny resemblance to the three physical layers that MacLean has detected in the structure of our triune brain.

The comparison does not stop there. Two thousand years earlier than Freud Hindu theorists developed a triune theory of mind, in which *manas*, the motor force, was lowest, *ahamkara* or the 'ego-maker' came next and higher, while the third and highest was *buddhi* or enlightened intellect. There are no crocodiles in the original Indian model, but there are horses. The senses are in fact compared to the spirited steeds that are liable to run out of control if not firmly restrained. It is the job of *manas* to be their reins, while *ahamkara* does the driving and *buddhi* the supervision. The parallelism with modern neurological findings is fascinating, the only difference being that the ancient Hindus added a fourth ingredient, *atman* ('self' or 'spirit'), an awareness of which greatly helps *buddhi* in its task. Neurophysiologists, however, do not normally venture into such additional and difficult dimensions as that.

The three-layered brain described by MacLean, however, is not the whole story. It has to be linked up with another set of recent investigations, also mainly in the United States, deriving from the work of Roger Sperry, Joseph Bogen and Michael Gazzaniga. These are the famous 'split-brain' studies, which have stirred up as much interest and concern as the triune brain. In this area of research the third and uppermost brain is the centre of attention. It is not by any means a unitary object; rather it consists almost entirely of two massive hemispherical sections.

There have been three main areas of investigation relating to those cerebral hemispheres. The initial experiments of Sperry, Bogen and Gazzaniga concerned first cats and then epileptics in whom the connection between the hemispheres had been severed. These were followed by complementary research into brain damage and its consequences together with detailed and varied studies of hemispheric specialization among 'normal' people, using carefully constructed and conducted tests relating to sight and hearing. The results of all three indicate that in human adults the two hemispheres *are* not only heavily specialized but – as the neurologist and computer scientist Ernest Kent puts it in *The Brains of Men and Machines* (1981) – there are 'two separate and individual conscious

intellects dwelling within the same head!' (and the exclamation mark
is his, one of very few in his sober study).

One hemisphere appears always to be dominant, and in most
people it is the left, almost invariably linked to the dominant right
hand. In it resides not only the controlling dexterity for that hand
but also the faculties of language, logical reasoning and mathematics
(whether or not these are formally refined and developed in our
systems of education). The minor hemisphere is deficient in these,
but competent in non-verbal reasoning – which includes the
mysterious quality called 'intuition' – as well as the ability to
recognize pictures and organize relations in space. Just as the two
lower brains are connected, so a thick bundle of nerves, the corpus
callosum, unites the two upper hemispheres; although evolution
since the Pleistocene did not achieve a strong low/high link-up,
it did manage to bind the hemispheres decently together. As a result
they are well integrated, but if the corpus callosum is cut the distinct
hemispheric personalities – talkative on the left, taciturn on the
right – will pursue their own interests. This can have bizarre
consequences, as for example when one hand might be instructed
by one brain centre to stop the other hand doing what *it* has been
told to do. This results in a struggle between the hands, the one
to carry on, the other to prevent it from carrying on. Inside the
skull in such situations the two hemispheres have no means of
consulting one another.

In the normal course of events, however, it is clear that the two
hemispheres interact intimately. In order, for example, to relate
words (left hemisphere) with diagrams (right hemisphere) as in
this book, a fair degree of balanced co-operation is essential, while
in the unitive play of metaphors and parables it is crucial, blending
language and image into one inner experience.

To sum up, then, we may conclude that there are in effect two
Beauties above to counterbalance the two Beasts below, and
although they look like twins these Beauties have different lines
of development and different work to do. As Hampden-Turner
points out, neither the other primates (like the monkeys, baboons,
chimpanzees and gorillas) nor small children have this hemispheric
specialization, and most investigators have attributed it to language
learning. The linguist John Lyons agrees, observing in *Language
and Linguistics* (1981) that lateralization, the separating out of the
distinct functions, relates to maturation 'in the sense that it is

genetically pre-programmed'. It all takes time, however, beginning around the child's second year and stabilizing anywhere between the age of five and the onset of puberty. Serious language acquisition in the child begins at the same time, while after the completion of lateralization it becomes progressively harder for us to acquire new languages with the consistent ease of childhood.

Even the most imaginative of ancient myth-makers or modern science-fiction writers could not have thought up this new model of the brain-cum-brains. A deep-down crocodile is embedded in a middle-level horse on whose back ride mirror-twins, the one on the left talkative and good with numbers, the one on the right silent but a wizard with hunches, images and space relations. Clearly, the actual talents of this neural composite vary greatly from person to person, but this does seem to be what nature/evolution has provided us with. And the surprise is that it comes as no surprise, when we consider the history of our species and of our attempts to explain and improve ourselves. This is demonstrated by the very ease with which one can bring in names from myth and legend to talk about Beauty and the Beast, and so forth, and the willingness of MacLean and the others to think in terms of 'design flaws' that are remarkably close to such ideas as 'original sin' and 'the old Adam'.

There *are* splits and discontinuities inside us. Mystics and philosophers have pointed to them in behavioural terms for centuries, and have offered cures for them. Yoga is probably the most powerful example of a variously organized set of systems for taking this heterogeneous mass inside our heads and 'integrating' it, which is effectively what the word *yoga* means: 'yoking' or 'harnessing' everything so that it all works decently together, the personality slowly learning to transcend its inner contradictions. All religions offer their adherents not just social cohesion and rules for daily conduct but also spiritual 'paths' to be followed that lead to unity, often symbolized as 'union with God'. All such processes are vividly summed up in the Californian idiom of 'getting your head together'.

Unitive thinking can in this context be regarded as improved programming for the four-in-one brain system (see Figure 12). Its purpose is – as it appears always to have been – the creation of 'integrated circuits' at a sufficiently high and powerful level to overcome the everyday problems that the lower Beasts and the

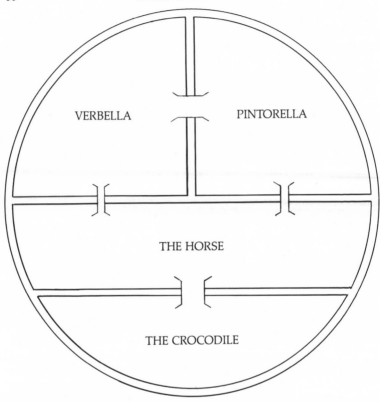

Figure 12. *A stylization of the four-in-one brain. A model of the compartments of the brain as described by such neurophysiological investigators as Paul MacLean and Roger Sperry. Below is the 'crocodile' of the brain stem, above it the 'horse' of the limbic system, and above them are the hemispheric 'twins' of the cerebral cortex, dominant and verbal on the left, minor and pictorial-cum-intuitive on the right. When yogis and mystics talk about 'integration' or 'union', these are the hardware components in each of us that have to begin to work together more smoothly.*

higher Beauties have in doing business with each other. One problem in the past, however, has been an anti-sensual tradition in many religions which has insisted that the lower Beasts are utterly to be rejected – that Flesh and the Devil are profoundly evil, separated off for ever from the Good and the Godly. In such extreme puritanical movements every effort has to be made to resist and suppress the forces down below, to curb one's desires until they disappear, to sublimate low into high – almost at all costs. This tradition has led to extreme ascetic practices throughout Asia and the Western World, has often encouraged 'holy' men to reject women as symbols of a defiling sexuality (Maya is female; Eve has the apple), has even encouraged self-starvation and ritual suicide in movements like those of the Jains of India and the Albigenses in France. It has also contributed to the ferocity of witch hunts and inquisitions and no doubt has a place in the Freudian guilts of many of us today, inheritors of a Calvinistic disapproval of everything below the navel, corresponding rather well in symbolic terms to MacLean's crocodile and horse.

Unitive thinking, following the more balanced aspects of traditional religion and mysticism, looks for a middle way between the extremes of ascetic withdrawal and sensual abandon. If you poison the beasts down below, then their corpses will in turn poison you. They are there to be ridden, have their own power, and *adequately reined in* can carry us a long way. The problem of adequately reining them in is the problem of the design flaw that MacLean, Koestler and Ardrey have pointed to: the slender links between beast and beauty. This, they are in effect saying, is why you can want to do something good and find yourself doing its opposite.

It is certainly a problem. A reptile is a reptile. It likes to lie in the sun and will snap at anything tasty that passes by. A horse is a horse, a proud and skittish creature, ready to rear up and flee, likely to lash out with its hoofs if it feels threatened, and to break a leg in panic. The cerebral twins also need to pay proper attention to each other, just like siblings in a nursery. The lucky twin with all the verbal and arithmetical capacities in her care needs to shut up now and then, letting her quiet but talented sister have a place in the limelight of civilization. It is quite a menagerie. But we need the deep and basic drives of the crocodile, the excitement of the horse, and the diverse talents of Verbella on the left and Pintorella on the right.

'Logic' lives with the verbal sister. What Edward de Bono calls 'lateral thinking' – creative, other-than-logical thinking – needs easy and flexible co-operation across both hemispheres. But *unitive* thinking is more than just cerebral activity on the upper levels. It has to inhabit and *inform* (to use the word in its older meaning of 'giving shape to') the whole of the brain ensemble and take everything into account. It must be a zoo-keeper for the crocodile, a master of equestrianship for the horse, a rational partner for Verbella and an exciting artist and acrobat in the company of Pintorella. *Then* it has to ensure that its zoo-keeping, horsemanship, rationalism and artistry flow together – and this as effortlessly as possible.

This is not easy, but it is not necessarily impossible, either. And, with the help of the neurological models that MacLean, Sperry and the other investigators are offering us, we ought to be in a better position today than our predecessors who experimented and speculated unitively in ancient India, Greece, Palestine, China and elsewhere.

Nor is it just the physiological and anatomical that prevents us from integrating ourselves. Language doesn't help, either. We have been told for centuries that each of us is an 'individual' – an indivisible unit. Mystics, philosophers and neurologists alike know that this is not so, but the word insists that it *is* so. It would be better if we called ourselves 'multiples', because we are rather like the demon in the Gospels whose name was Legion. All of us are capable of lop-sided growth among our various components, and few if any escape from some degree of imbalance. Then there is the additional conundrum that we either have no clear idea of how to integrate the various parts of our personalities, or we have too many competing systems to choose from: traditional religion, one or more psychotherapies, and a bit of Eastern promise in the form of yoga or Zen. Finally, there are the reasons that derive from upbringing, history and culture. We may not want to be or to look eccentric, may have repressed various aspects of ourselves to fit in with other people, may have a cultural bias towards this or that preference in thinking and behaving, *and – worst of all – may not even know it.*

We also experience a variety of discontinuities in the way we have learned to think and to use language. For example, 'the brain' itself does not figure very much in the history of thinking about thinking. In that context, 'mind' is the king, and mind has not always had a precise location. It might be in the head, but it has also been in some cultures located in the heart, or in both head and heart, contrasting the intellect and the emotions. In addition, it may be treated as an aspect of 'spirit' or 'soul', something inhabiting the body rather than of the body – something essentially non-physical, as in the Latin adage *mens sana in corpore sano* ('a healthy mind in a healthy body'), where 'body' must be taken to include 'brain'.

In dealing with all such expressions we are once again in the situation of thinking about the seven-day week. Mostly, we don't think about either the week or the brain or the mind. We simply accept them all as solid, as given – and, although they may have been given to us, they are not necessarily solid concepts at all. The kluuls certainly found this to be the case when they were sitting in their starship, behind their visibility barrier, observing the creatures on the planet Earth. After they had studied our systems for measuring time they went on to analyse our assumptions about personality and existence, and that really stumped them.

You see, they discovered that the dominant civilization on the planet is not even sure what a 'body' is. If we say, 'Mind is distinct from body' then we mean that mind is intangible and the physical part of us is tangible (etc.), and goes from crown to feet. But if we say, 'He was killed in battle – they found his body but not his head', then the crown-to-feet coverage isn't true any more, because one *can* have a 'headless body'. Next, people can say, 'There are marks on her body, but not on her legs and arms', in which case not just the head goes but so do all four limbs, and we are left with a 'limbless, headless body', which is also an acceptable phrase. This greatly surprised the kluuls, for whom of course their nearest equivalent, *phraash*, simply means 'scale-sheath'. It refers to every observable part of a kluul except the eyes, which are gateways to the inner kluul.

They next looked at what was not the body, and found a different kind of chaos, from a kluul point of view. Whereas 'body' could cover anything with or without the head and/or limbs, the other side of existence was covered by a whole raft of terms such as 'mind', 'psyche', 'soul' and 'spirit'. How the one could be distinguished from the others was not at all clear, and the Earthlings seemed to get a great deal of satisfaction from failing to distinguish them, or from not noticing that they needed some kind of separating out. Of those Earthlings who did think about such matters, some said they were all quite distinct from each other and the body, some said that only three exist ('soul' and 'spirit' being the same thing), some said that only two exist ('psyche', 'soul' and 'spirit' all being the same thing), some that only one exists (all of them being different words for the same thing), and some saying that none exist, all of them referring to the electrochemical froth given off by the brain while hard at work.

This confounded the observers from Arcturus, for whom there were only two terms, *phraash* for the outer kluul or 'scale-sheath' and *maphríish* for the inner kluul or 'sheathed one'. When an investigator came up with yet another human term – 'consciousness' – the whole investigation was called off, and in their thesaurus of Earthisms all such words were simply glossed as 'kinds of *maphríish*'.

In a sense, the kluuls (in this area at least) are luckier than we are: they carry less linguistic luggage. Our luggage is rich and interesting, but it promotes confusion as often as it encourages communication and comprehension. But it is just possible that this age-old conundrum *can* be simplified, using a modern analogy – or at least, in unitive terms, can be re-seen from a fresh point of view.

The world of the computer is divided into two areas: hardware and software. Hardware is the solidly physical portion of any computer system, including its electric-cum-electronic devices, circuits and drives. In contrast, software is 'those components of a computer system that are intangible rather than physical' (*Dictionary of Computing*, Oxford, 1986). Computers are therefore dualistic; without the hardware Yang co-operating with the software Yin, no computational circle would be complete. This is pretty close to what the mystics have always said about *us*, and what the kluuls appear to be saying too. We, like the much simpler computer, are two-sided beings. Leaving the mass of the body to one side for the moment, we can say that in our lives the physical brain and its network of nerves is the neurological hardware that runs us, while everything else, whatever we call it – 'mind', 'psyche', 'soul', 'spirit', etc. – is the psychological software. The one is tangible and inspectable, part of the body, while the other is intangible and *not* directly available for inspection.

It is, however, there. Humanity has always been conscious of it, just as conscious of it as the kluuls, and even we have talked about the eyes as 'the windows of the soul'. One very ancient school of thought says that mentality or spirit comes from elsewhere and for a time inhabits and co-occurs with a body, while one very modern school of thought says that everything arises materially from the body, this intangible software included. At present, neither strict religion nor strict science can prove its case in terms that would stand up in the court of everyday reality. It might be better if they did not even try, as things stand. Each has a tantalizing case, but neither has the final evidence, both ultimately depending upon an act of faith on the part of their adherents. That act of faith – in strict spiritualism or strict materialism – may be useful for the individuals involved, but this usefulness does not make it other than an act of faith.

We *are*, however, left with what matters – the dualism of hardware and software, or, if you will, the existence of a 'hard' reality of facts, sticks and stones, flesh and bone, and a 'soft' reality of consciousness, ideas, inner images, inner speech and writing, logic and fantasy, emotion and intuition. Each is equally 'real', is dependent upon the other, affects and interacts with the other, and does so whether we choose to operate a spiritualist, a materialist, or any other model of how they came to *be* together. For its existence as we perceive and conceive it, human 'personality' needs both the hard outer and soft inner aspects.

To return to the computer analogy, we can take a closer look at the idea of programming. Software is something that people slot into the hardware of computation, or may arrange to have permanently available in tandem with the hardware. This does not much matter. What matters more is the nature and the flexibility of the intangibles that operate the machines. Some of these relate directly to basic maintenance, and in human terms these are the programs at the level of the crocodile and the horse, taking care of the autonomic nervous system with its breathing and heartbeat, muscular action and digestive processes (etc.); others relate to instinctual drives and emotional responses, and blend in with the everyday thought processes of the twins Verbella and Pintorella. But the higher up the human mechanism one goes the more flexibility one finds. At the level of the automatic, there is little flexibility, although even there one can control the breath and even affect the beating of the heart (as yoga has amply demonstrated). At the level of the instinctual and emotional we do not need to be mass-murderers or constantly throw tantrums (as every system of human self-control from Stoicism onward demonstrates). And at the level of the truly human we are born into and can acquire any language on earth, as well as develop well enough to handle a wide range of social and professional activities, from driving buses to singing pop songs to performing in arias to analysing the brain.

What this points to is a remarkable potentiality, the virtual cliché that we never exploit our mental resources to the full. Unitive thinking is a new name for – and perhaps a new presentation of – an age-old invitation to recognize the diversity of brain and mind, and to explore their potential more fully than we usually do. It doesn't matter whether the idea of exploring and developing one's potential is a cliché or not. It only became a cliché because it was a good idea in the first place, and what does matter is doing it. In turn, doing it matters because, whether we like to admit it or not, quality matters.

Follow-up to Chapter 5

Figure 13 is almost a cliché these days, in illustrating the optical illusion and challenging children to concentrate. This cliché status, however, arises from the very potency of the imagery involved. Have a look at it in relation to the invitations on the next page.

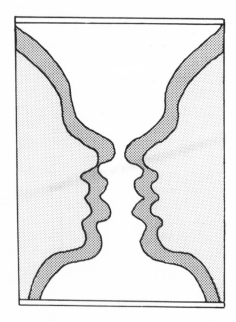

Figure 13.

○ How many Yin–Yang relationships can you find in the diagram? Come back to it afresh several times until you are sure of your total.
○ How can one use the diagram to symbolize the double vision of the Maya/Brahman contrast at the end of Chapter 3? (You can use the idea of 'backgrounding' and 'foregrounding' images as an aid here.)

● Proverbs and idioms may become worn with over-use, but they still contain powerful – and often unitive – implications. Play about with these:

Look before you leap.
Between the devil and the deep blue sea (*British*).
Between a rock and a hard place (*American*).
In a cleft stick.
On the horns of a dilemma.
Don't count your chickens before they're hatched.
Don't cross your bridges before you come to them.

● After studying our systems for measuring time and describing our personalities, the kluuls from Arcturus moved on to our colour code. Theirs is rather different. For them, colours relate primarily to the signalling tints on their scales for the different phases that they go through as they mature. Thus, 'red' they associate with youthful liveliness and inexperience, 'yellow' with mating and brooding, and 'green' with prestige, maturity and serenity. So how would they respond to these?

○ the saffron robe of an Eastern monk or nun
○ a red herring; being green with envy; and a yellow streak
○ traffic lights

● the imagery in Figure 12 derives from the imagery employed by the neurophysiologist Paul MacLean himself in describing the layers of the brain. I have also quoted Robert Ardrey where he says that the upper and lower brains do not have the same language. Do the images, however, offer a means of communication of any kind between our inner Mirror Twins, Horses and Crocodiles – or even the possibility of controlling them all better?

● The left hemisphere of the brain controls the right side of the head and body, while the right hemisphere controls the left side. The feet are controlled from the top of the cortex of the brain, while the muscles of the face are controlled from the bottom of the cortex. What unitive principle is therefore built into our physical foundations?

Figure 14. *Homunculus.*

● Homunculus (Figure 14) is a somewhat bizarre dwarf created as a response to the pioneering research into the brain undertaken by the Canadian, Wilder Penfield. It shows the physical proportions of our heads and bodies *if* their size related precisely to the amount of brain space given to our various parts. How do you feel about being – in neural terms – all hands, feet and mouth?

● Now that you know how weird you are, what steps do you reckon could be taken to benefit from the knowledge – assuming, of course, that any benefit at all is possible.

6

Ladders of the Mind

In the land of Urbania the trains all run on time and everything is looked after by the National Board of Benefactors.

The Benefactors know – and have known for centuries – what is best for the citizens of Urbania, or at least what is best for most of the people most of the time. They have also tended to believe – although occasionally they have had heated debates on the subject – that the mass of the citizens haven't the slightest idea what is good either for them or for the nation as a whole. The people therefore need to be guided, and who better to guide them than those who have always had the greatest happiness of the greatest number constantly in mind?

Everything, so the Benefactors tell anyone who will listen, is a matter of education and social progress. Once upon a time – would anyone believe it today? – Urbania was a savage and chaotic place, full of dissatisfaction, violence, free-thinking, disease and unreason. Then the Great Enlightenment came and the Basic Problem was uncovered. That problem, of course, was raw human nature, a wayward quality that human beings could well do without. Raw human nature was like a wilderness; well-governed human nature was like a beautiful garden, and the Benefactors came together to cultivate that garden.

Gardens, however, sometimes have weeds in them, and the weeds in the Urbanian garden were the three great classes of Difficult People. The Benefactors, however, created three institutions to take care of the three problem groups, and these institutions function smoothly, by and large, to this day. The first of the institutions is the *Prison*, a place to hold and treat those Difficult People found guilty of crime. The second of the institutions is the *Hospital*, a place to hold and treat those Difficult People found guilty of illness. And the third of the institutions is the *School*, a place to hold and treat those Difficult People found guilty of both youth and ignorance. It is, say the Benefactors, these three institutions which mark the greatness of modern Urbania and which have taken its citizens from the depths of chaos to the heights of good order and social harmony.

The three great institutions work so well – most of the time – because they are all built in accordance with the fundamental principle of Urbanian life, the square. The nearer that everything comes to rectilinear perfection, the better life is for everyone, or so the theory goes. Roundness, though of course it is not outlawed, is therefore reduced to a minimum. Thus, the three institutions in their various realizations throughout the land tend – like so much else in Urbania – to be oblong: the squares of cell and classroom, ward and wardrobe, the rectangles of doors, windows, corridors, vestibules, stairways, elevators, tables, desks, cupboards, lockers and boxes. On many a wall are affixed neat sheets of paper listing the rules and regulations appropriate to a place, pinned up squarely where everybody with the ability to read can peruse them.

Time is marked off not just in minutes and hours but re-squared into periods for this and periods for that: 'Time to get up, 324!' – 'Time for your aperient, Mrs Gummidge!' – 'Time for your Arithmetic class, young Postlethwaite!' It is all so organized that, just as the Benefactors intend, the inmates of the three institutions soon become ill at ease in surroundings that are not square and are uncertain what to do with time that has the wrong shape.

Although it is not widely conceded, however, there are some flies in the benevolent ointment of Urbania. Whisper it, but many of the Three Ps – the Prisoners, Patients and Pupils – do not always allow themselves to benefit from their time in one or other institution, a fact which has occasioned great sadness and occasionally bouts of black rage among the Benefactors. Many criminals go back to crime when their time is up inside. Many patients stubbornly remain ill – and even elect to die – both inside and outside their clinics. And large numbers of pupils, although they are gratifyingly and permanently cured of their youth, are not at all cured of their ignorance. The Benefactors and their friends, however, have found the ideal solution to this problem: they build larger institutions, keep more people in them for longer periods, and declare that the institutions mark the greatness of Urbania, having taken the citizens from the depths of chaos to the heights of good order and social harmony. Anyone supposing otherwise is quietly taken off to a fourth institution that no one ever talks about. Those who have ears to hear, let them hear.

So much for satire. The only problem with a parable cast in the form of satire is that it is strong and uncompromising stuff, like Orwell's *Animal Farm* or Huxley's *Brave New World*. It takes an extreme position to make certain points rather bluntly. It is designed both to provoke thought and to leave the receiver of its message disturbed. It is polemical and propagandistic, because its 'secret' message is the opposite of what it seems to be saying.

In the case of satirizing Western city life and its institutions, and in particular its processes of education and social service, the danger is that it misrepresents all the good and caring people – the *genuinely* benevolent – who look after our schools, hospitals, prisons and other public services. They may react unhappily to the very idea that they could be Fascists and the fellow-travellers of Fascists – and rightly too. Nevertheless, many of them are fully aware of a curious conflict in the assumptions that underlie the prison system (is it rehabilitation, or revenge, or just a trash-can for misfits of various kinds?), the hospital system (is it Florence Nightingale militarism, and no nonsense about it, or a place for healing and compassion?), and the educational system (is it a place where young people grow and express themselves, or is it penal servitude throughout childhood and adolescence, in the service of a national ideology, however clearly or fuzzily worked out?).

When he wrote *Brave New World* in the 1930s, Aldous Huxley was uneasily aware both of the rise of the Fascist states in Europe and the ways in which science – that dream of human betterment – could be turned into an engine of eugenics and euthanasia in the service of new supermen and master races. Fifty years ago, long before the word 'clone' had become daily currency, Huxley imagined a future World State where the solution to the problem of human nature lay in 'Bokanovsky's Process':

'One egg, one embryo, one adult – normality. But a Bokanovskified egg will bud, will proliferate, will divide. From eight to ninety-six buds, and every bud will grow into a perfectly formed embryo, and every embryo into a full-sized adult. Making ninety-six human beings grow where only one grew before. Progress.'

Huxley's is one extreme, where technology is brought in to sort us out. Orwell's is another, in which 'thought police' can persuade us, subtly or by coercion and torture, to believe that black is white, if the State so wishes. What they are both highlighting is the relationship between ideology and politics on the one hand and education on the other, points strung out along a hazardous continuum. The Urbanian vignette adds the clash between state and individual, institution and ideal – between Those Who Know Best (or think they do) and Those Who are Ignorant (and are assumed to have no means of escaping that ignorance save through the programmes and policies of one kind of Benefactor or another). It is a perennial conundrum. Plato, who so well illustrated higher knowledge with his Simile of the Cave, also offered the world his Republic, with its philosopher kings and its 'guardians' – raising the chilling question of who would guard the guardians. His intentions were excellent, but what he proposed was a vision of government and good order that has always appealed to people who like their institutional gardens to be entirely clear of weeds.

Ancient India is an object lesson to the whole world of what happened when social planners collided with determined eccentrics who wanted nothing to do with those social plans. The story began over three thousand years ago, when the Aryan clans came down with their horses and wagons from Central Asia and spread slowly in the ensuing centuries across the Indian subcontinent. They were a fairer-skinned people than the Dravidian races whom they found already living along the rivers Indus and Ganges. Their very name for themselves – the *Arya* or Noble Ones – suggests the extent to which they saw themselves as natural aristocrats. Like the Normans in England, they became the upper classes of their new lands, and just as the Normans had their tensions between cleric and knight so the Aryans had a built-in tension between the caste of *brahmin* priests and the caste of *kshatriya* warriors and governors. Below these were the *vaishya* peasants and artisans, and below them again the dark multitudes who were either just within the caste system as *shudras* or for ever outside it as the *avarnas* – outcaste, untouchable and even, for some, unseeable.

This stratification of society has been in place ever since, and even the secular government of today's Republic of India has not been able – or may not have even wanted – to legislate the differences away. The caste system, like any other enormous social institution, has both its acceptable and its unacceptable faces. It is complex beyond belief, and any simple description of it serves to distort it in some way. Within it there are exceptions to every rule, but by and large, when all the qualifications have been made, it has been and is one of the world's most massively successful programmes of social engineering. The old high castes are still high, and the old low castes and outcastes are still low. Much of that marvellous mass of cults and religions called Hinduism serves to buttress caste – the holy Vedas themselves serve to justify it, compiled as they were long ago by self-assured brahmins – and provides the ideology that keeps this great social engine going.

The caste system exists in the real world because brahmins long ago organized a world-view so powerful that it dominates the minds of millions. That world-view proposes a wheel of births and deaths, everyone bound on that wheel, everyone constrained to do his or her duty by caste and kin, by ancestors and children, in the hope that enough merit will be accumulated to make the *next* life easier. Progress up the social – and racial – ladder across lives is painfully slow, but it is, so tradition says, the only sure progress. At least there *is* a ladder, a ladder of the mind so constructed as to convince the masses that the best thing to do is to conform, to do one's duty, to pray to the gods, and to improve one's *karma*. It is an invitation to ascend the ladder so slowly that one hardly ascends it at all, and the great institutions and their preservers are safe for yet another generation.

And yet there has always been a radical refusal to go along with this view of things, a slender thread often mingled with the main threads of caste and conformity, and that thread puts the individual first rather than the community, asking people to think quite differently. Nowadays, as Indian philosophy and yoga, it appears to be hopelessly mixed in with conventional static Hinduism, and yet . . .

The revolt appears to have begun when certain kshatriyas – irked by the pretensions of the brahmins to a godlike status and to all knowledge and power – blended their own ideas with others that

they found among the darker and older population. Out of this
new blend came not only some of the most powerful images and
practices of popular non-brahminical Hinduism but also the
philosophy of the Upanishads, in which brahmins are often shown
humbly receiving a higher knowledge from kshatriya princes. Out
of it also came that archetypal ideological rebel, Prince Gautama
Siddhartha Shakyamuni of Magadha, who is believed to have lived
from 563 to 483 BC and is still one of the world's most famous
figures – the Buddha.

His system was anti-brahminical and neutral towards the gods,
and urged its adherents to work diligently towards their own
salvation. Buddhism and other anti-brahminical movements
emphasized personal ladders of the mind as opposed to the static
social hierarchy. They were negative at heart, describing this world
of caste and tribulation as a place of suffering from which the wise
sought to escape entirely. The brahminical wheel of births and
deaths they saw as simply prolonging the agony – and they offered
one thing that had many names: *nirvana, moksha, mukti, ananda,
kaivalya* and *samadhi*. That thing was freedom, a freedom of the
spirit, something higher than caste, better than life itself, and
achievable not through priestly intercession but by slow and steady
self-improvement. You could, said such sages as Gautama the
Buddha and Patanjali, the father of Classical Yoga, evolve by means
of certain assumptions and techniques until you were truly free
and enlightened, and beholden to none for that freedom. Indeed,
pursue it far enough and you would recognize both the illusion
of the world and the oneness that lay behind it, both of them
unperceived by those who were engaged in the pursuit of earthly
power, whether priestly or military.

The Buddha offered his followers a system to follow that is called
the Noble Eight-Fold Path, while Patanjali offered his followers
the classical Eight-Limb Yoga. Where the conventional strata of
society and life are static, both of these systems propose something
dynamic, and the markedly similar rungs of their dynamic
psychological ladders are shown in Figure 15.

The metaphor of ladders or paths is of no great importance,
except that human life in many languages is saturated with images
of paths and journeys, ascents and heavenly quests that emphasize
'steps' of one kind or another, excelsior stages going ever onward
and upward. The important thing here is the individualism

The Noble Eight-Fold Path or *arya-ashthangika-marga* of Gautama the Buddha

The Eight-Limb Yoga or *ashthanga-yoga* of Patanjali

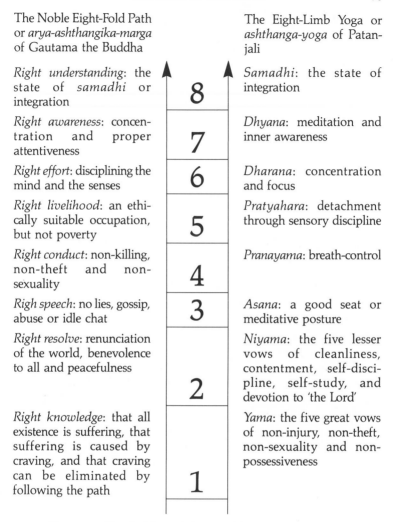

Right understanding: the state of *samadhi* or integration

8

Samadhi: the state of integration

Right awareness: concentration and proper attentiveness

7

Dhyana: meditation and inner awareness

Right effort: disciplining the mind and the senses

6

Dharana: concentration and focus

Right livelihood: an ethically suitable occupation, but not poverty

5

Pratyahara: detachment through sensory discipline

Right conduct: non-killing, non-theft and non-sexuality

4

Pranayama: breath-control

Righ speech: no lies, gossip, abuse or idle chat

3

Asana: a good seat or meditative posture

Right resolve: renunciation of the world, benevolence to all and peacefulness

2

Niyama: the five lesser vows of cleanliness, contentment, self-discipline, self-study, and devotion to 'the Lord'

Right knowledge: that all existence is suffering, that suffering is caused by craving, and that craving can be eliminated by following the path

1

Yama: the five great vows of non-injury, non-theft, non-sexuality and non-possessiveness

Figure 15. *Two ladders of the mind from ancient India.*

involved, because we are often taught to think of the East as collective rather than individualistic, while the West is the place where, from the time of the ancient Greeks, people have been developing the idea of individuals and their rights. So individualistic, however, are the essential tenets of such movements as Buddhism and yoga that they were often feared by the brahmins and others among the orthodox because they threatened the social law and family life. Men and women under such systems could and did turn their backs on family obligations – including that most important obligation of all, to have children – and by becoming lone wanderers or *sadhus* stepped outside the caste system.

Eventually the system absorbed them, using them as a social safety valve that permitted certain people to use spiritual goals as a means of bypassing conformity, while the bulk of society did as it had been told to do. Curiously enough, that tactful book the *Bhagavad-Gita* is evidence of the desire for compromise between society and eccentric, between the public and the personal. In praising everything, and in giving its blessing both to the fair-skinned brahmins and the dark god Krishna it helped to create modern India, in which inertia and experimentation coexist uneasily but do coexist.

This is rather similar to the situation of religious mystics and other visionaries within societies elsewhere. The Roman Catholic Church from medieval times onward has been rather like the Hindu social engine: arguing for stability and obedience, seeking not to disturb the faith of the simple. Within such a vast bureaucracy centred upon the Vatican the best saints have often seemed to be those who were safely dead and canonized – indeed, unlike Hinduism, where one can meet a saint quite easily, it is axiomatic that one *has* to be dead before one can be a candidate for sanctification. It is retroactive legislation, and the eccentric individual no longer disturbs the peace. Other eccentrics, however, whose views on religion, society and science disturbed the peace were not so easily handled, and were persecuted and died in all manner of inhumane ways. But none of that has ever stopped the mystically inclined from being themselves. Often loners to start with, they would either pursue their visions and insights more privately within society, or take themselves off into hermit-like isolation, or into a monastic order that would support their lifestyle in a politically acceptable way.

All of which concerns both mass education and personal self-improvement, or some mixture of the two. All of it is environmental; that is, one has been born into a society, has been stamped with its picture of things, and then begins to think about that picture and about the larger life that it purports to describe. Either one accepts the picture offered or one explores further, maybe even to the mystic's stage that is beyond all pictures. In the process one may come up against the establishment or may learn to live with the establishment and persuade it to live with you. Any ladder of the mind that is climbed, however, is one's own, either in co-operation with society or to some degree independently of it. This is the traditional situation, and it still largely holds true, because independent – and unitively inclined – thinkers now as in the past make compromises with the world around them just like everybody else. The only difference today is that the world pictures offered by our various great societies are less secure than they used to be, because we see enough of them to allow for comparisons, some favourable, some not so favourable. There is more choice, and that very choice breeds a greater willingness on many people's parts to think independently – and *unitively*, because they want to make sense of the whole, not just of the parts offered to them in childhood.

And that is where we move over the line from environment into biology, from adult thought into the world of the child.

At first sight, Darwin's theory of evolution is an entirely different subject from unitive thinking, Buddhism and yoga. It is more, however, than a biological theory with broader human implications. It is also, for one thing, saturated with metaphors and can be read like a parable. In it the mysterious quality isolated as 'life' *rises* from the primordial slime and turns itself into a *tree of life* (which is a very ancient symbol indeed). This tree has many branches, some *lower*, some *higher*, and something within the sap-like flow of life has been propelling itself ever higher, pushing blindly through all sorts of natural selection – billions of choices over millions of years – until we, *Homo sapiens*, appeared on the scene and began to think about it all, and talk about trees of life, classifications of species, their origins, and ultimately their evolution.

Although many scientists insist that the theory of evolution ought not to be judged by its symbolism, ought instead to be seen for what it is, a probabilistic machine operating on its own for millions of years, people inevitably ask: Is it *going* anywhere?

The answer is often 'Yes', and the direction is usually symbolized as 'up'. It is therefore another ladder, both of nature and the mind. Jacob Bronowski brought out a successful popular account of evolution in 1973, whose title says it all (and in a traditionally sexist way): *The Ascent of Man*. The West's belief in 'progress' is underlined in it, and the biologists' ladder or tree of species continues to be one of the most powerful mental images ever invented. However, just like the Hindu ladder of reincarnation it operates so slowly that, for us, it might as well not be operating at all. Whatever progress we make through all the aeons is bound to be too slow for any single generation – you or me – to notice. Both Sri Aurobindo in India and Pierre Teilhard de Chardin in Europe offer us some consolation all the same: Human we may be now, they say, but slowly we are evolving towards the divine. Our race will one day give birth to gods, and there are those among us – great souls of various kinds – who are forerunners of those gods.

This is a heady thought, and yet if we are going upwards where else is there to go but towards divinity, about the only concept we have of creatures higher (and better) than ourselves? Evolution is seen as a kind of schooling, or, as Teilhard has put it in *The Future of Man* (1959), 'for practical purposes, education is a universal biological function, coextensive with the totality of the living world'.

The Swiss developmental psychologist Jean Piaget was, by and large, more interested in children than in adults, and as far as I know was not overly concerned with the issues that Bronowski and Teilhard were interested in. He was a biologist, took an interest in psychoanalysis, but spent most of his long life investigating children, 'haunted', as he put it, 'by the idea of discovering a sort of embryology of intelligence'.

In this he was concerned with what happens as children mature; the condition of adults did not concern him, and the future of the species was not within his field of inquiry. In addition, he was not disposed like Sigmund Freud or Carl Jung, or indeed Charles Darwin, to create theories on a grand scale. However, for more than 60 years he studied all kinds of children in all kinds of situations, concluding that youngsters reason differently from adults and have different views of the world. Indeed, he averred, small children have a primitive aspect to them, and it takes time to develop such things as the skills of abstract thinking. To put it crudely, for Piaget there was a sense that in some respects children as they mature recapitulate the maturation of the species. He concluded that the human organism learns partly by nature, partly by nurture, and does so through four clearly discernible stages, as follows.

1 *The sensorimotor stage*, from birth to about two years of age, when the child works via direct contact with objects in the world, becoming aware that, for example, they still exist when out of sight.

2 *The pre-operational stage*, from around two to around seven, when the child begins to create a mental model of the world 'out there', an inner landscape in which there are contradictions of all sorts arising from experience, needing to be resolved by conclusions from further experience. Things like quantities, proportions and perspective are troublesome, and logic is good as far as it goes, although the landscape has a magical quality, as for example when children believe that the sun in the sky follows them around. It is a fantasy time.

3 *The concrete operational stage*, from around seven to eleven or twelve, when the young person learns to handle such culture-linked matters as concepts of space and sequence, weight, size, mass and time. The semantic space of the inner landscape is being enriched all the time. Language is now fully established (as we now know, in one dominant hemisphere of the brain), and logic is gaining ground over fantasy.

4 *The formal operational stage*, from around twelve onward, when abstraction becomes easier and problem-solving that involves abstraction and generalization becomes established, along with the use of language to talk about language and thought.

This is a four-container model of the continuum of a child's life, and is evidently an accurate picture across cultures as well as in the world of the European children who were Piaget's closest contacts. There also appears to be a fair correlation between what Piaget concluded from his studies of and projects with youngsters and the stages of maturation of the brain, and my description of the four Piagetian levels is a present-day catch-all rather than a rigorous reproduction of his own position at various points in the past. My purpose in outlining it here, however, is less to draw attention to Piaget as a psychologist of childhood than to show what someone else has done with the *ideas* of Piaget in relation – intriguingly enough – to the ideas of the metaphysical mavericks of ancient India.

The adapter and extender of Piaget is the Canadian psychologist Herbert Koplowitz, who in the 1970s quite simply took Piaget beyond childhood, and beyond the conventional. Whereas both Piaget and other investigators and commentators in the same area assumed that Stage 4's formal operations set us up for life, Koplowitz has asked whether there might not be more to life and human effort than simply passing through the barrier from concrete to abstract. In other words, there might be more to our lives than a recapitulation of past human stages through the animalian first stage to the animistic second stage and then the feet-on-the-ground world of common sense that is finally augmented by higher reasoning. Koplowitz has argued that *two* other stages can be detected.

5 *The stage of 'systems thinking',* in which the individual comes to appreciate the interconnection of things and the existence of multiple systems, not just one set of events or causes and effects. In commenting on Koplowitz in *The Aquarian Conspiracy* of 1980, Marilyn Ferguson notes: 'Conventional science assumes that cause and effect can be clearly separated and does not reach the level of Systems Thinking.' If that is so, then the bulk of humanity is unlikely to get there either, and common sense tells us – though as far as I know Piaget did not enlarge upon the matter – there are many people who only have a tenuous grip on the abstract thinking of his Stage 4.

6 *The stage of 'unitary operational thought',* in which people become aware of their own social and cultural conditioning. In it they appreciate that the way in which we perceive the external world is only one of the many possible ways. Koplowitz gives the example of opposites which can be construed as interdependent rather than as separate – much as I have discussed them under the unitive options of the split-circle diagrams. 'The Unitary thinker', says Ferguson, 'is to a Formal Operational adult as that adult is to a child.' Koplowitz explicitly ties his higher levels of operation to the mystical traditions of Tao and yoga, and supposes that these 'may offer the most thoroughly developed bodies of Unitary Operational Thought'.

Inevitably, if one proposes two attainable stages beyond the four hammered out empirically by Piaget, but assumes that they are not easily accessible to the mass of humanity, then there are several consequences. Firstly, the argument goes back down the line, as

I did above, and must argue that for some of us the various Piagetian stages are not necessarily accessible either. In other words, some people may not, for whatever reasons, get beyond Stages 1, 2, or 3. Secondly, if we are really talking about a continuum rather than strict containers, then we must imagine human beings around the world strung out along the continuum of self-growth part-way through Stage 3, well into 4, getting on into 5, and so forth. Thirdly, to systematize this too firmly and to devise, say, tests to establish who is where is to create a rather dangerous new hierarchy of Those Who Know Less and Those Who Know More. Fourthly, if there are techniques which help in the development of abstract thought – and we know that there are many such techniques – then there should also be techniques that develop systems thinking and unitary operationalism. Many of the techniques in this book would belong among them, and ought presumably to be made as widely available as possible to those who want to try them out. The danger, however, in any ladder-like list is that those who perceive themselves to be higher up that ladder may disdain those below or at best patronize them.

The theory, however, remains intriguing. My own inclination is to accept the six benchmarks (four from Piaget and two from Koplowitz) as useful constructs whose reality – physical, neurological, or psychological – may yet be firmly established. They harmonize well with the theory of evolution and suggest that we could indeed be going somewhere describable as 'up' – as long as the idea of 'super-beings' who can decide the fate of 'lesser mortals' does not become too attractive to those who think they belong at Stages 5 and 6.

In addition, I also suspect that we do not simply pass from stage to stage, leaving each behind like an old skin shed by a kluul or a snake. Rather, we take all our baggage with us, much as, in transactional analysis, Eric Berne and Thomas A. Harris have indicated that we take all the baggage of Child and Parent with us as we seek to become Adult. We also retrogress too, and oftener than we would like to admit – sliding back to the basics of Stage 1, enjoying or terrified by the fantasies of Stage 2, and being as illogical as we like in the incomplete world between Stages 3 and 4. Such a possibility certainly would account for the behaviour of many a giant of perception – Eastern guru or Western intellectual – who may have reached the topmost unitary rung only to fall heavily back into egotism and greed. The examples are common enough.

My suspicion that this is so is buttressed by another ladder model, this time Abraham Maslow's. As a founder of humanistic psychology and an inquirer into the nature of mysticism, Maslow created a five-point scale that has much in common with the Piaget–Koplowitz scheme. He has argued that human beings consolidate themselves at each point of the scale as they satisfy certain needs. As each 'lower' need is taken care of, so a 'higher' need presents itself and takes charge of the human organism. In their rising sequence, these five needs are:

1 At the physiological level, the need for food, drink and exercise (and, most basically, one might add, for air).
2 At the level of safety or security, the need for shelter and a degree of order (but how much order, and imposed by whom, always remains a problem).
3 At the social level, the need to belong, to be accepted and to be loved (for which one has to make concessions and learn to negotiate).
4 At the level of esteem, the need for acknowledgement, for status and for a degree of prestige.
5 At the level of *self-actualization* (the quintessential Maslovian phrase), the need for fulfilment and growth.

For Maslow, all of these needs are nested one inside the other, all simultaneously present but latent in every human being; they have nothing to do with ability or capacity of body or mind, but a lot to do with survival and success as an organism. Circumstances can just as easily cause someone to revert to a lower level of need (in a crisis) as to ascend to a higher level of need (when everything is going well). At the fifth level Maslow's metaphor is related to scaling mountains, because there one has 'peak experiences' of a mystical nature, varying according to one's experience, culture and expectations – and if one is persistent, consistent and fortunate those peak experiences may smooth out into a high 'plateau effect'. As Maslow puts it, when discussing the importance of sexuality in *Religions, Values and Peak Experiences* in 1964:

'Such perceptions and awarenesses should be able to help any male and any female to experience the transcendent and unitive, both in oneself and in the other. In this way, the eternal becomes visible *in* and *through* the particular, the symbolic and platonic can be experienced *in* and *through* the concrete instance, the sacred can fuse with the profane, and one can transcend the universe of time and space while being in it.'

There is an admirable inclusiveness in this. It does away with the need for a metaphor of climbing and height, even though it still uses such words as 'transcend' and 'transcendent'. All of the levels, however labelled, are there together, at one. It recalls the warnings of the Buddhist monk and the yogi that the rules of the Eight-Fold Path and of Eight-Limb Yoga are not parts of paths or the limbs of anything. Rather, they are skills and qualities to be acquired how one will but to be managed all together, simultaneously. You climb these ladders of mind and spirit in order to realize that there was nothing to climb. To fall in love with the ladder and with oneself for having climbed it is the biggest mistake one could make.

Follow-up to Chapter 6

● Below is a Zen verse, slightly adapted from *Games Zen Masters Play* (the translations of R. H. Blyth selected and edited by Robert Sohl and Audrey Carr). How might one relate it to this chapter?

Walking along the edge of a sword –
Running over thin ice;
Not using a ladder,
Climbing precipices handless.

● All social institutions appear to have their acceptable and unacceptable faces. We have taken a look at the people's paradise called Urbania. Have you ever been there?

● The Urbanians 'soon become ill at ease in surroundings that are not square and are uncertain what to do with time that has the wrong shape'. How about you?

● In *Games People Play: The Basic Handbook of Transactional Analysis*, Eric Berne says: 'Structure-hunger has the same survival value as stimulus-hunger. Stimulus-hunger and recognition-hunger express the need to avoid sensory and emotional starvation, both of which lead to biological deterioration. Structure-hunger expresses the need to avoid boredom, and Kierkegaard has pointed out the evils which result from unstructured time. If it persists for any length of time, boredom becomes synonymous with emotional starvation and can have the same consequences.'

Is it also possible, however, for someone – perhaps a prisoner, a patient or a pupil, for instance – to become bored and hungry for stimulus *inside* a thoroughly structured world of space and time?

● Transactional analysis is a school of therapy which does not use the images of ladder or path. Rather, it focuses on the relationships among three 'ego-states': the Child, the Parent and the Adult. In terms of these ego-states, it discusses our well-being – yours and mine – in terms of being OK or not OK. The four options are:

I'm not OK – You're OK   (I'm low and you are high)
I'm not OK – You're not OK   (We are both low)
I'm OK – You're not OK   (I am high and you are low)
I'm OK – You're OK   (We are both high – and secure)

In terms of such relationships and the three ego-states, people play games with each other, games that can be safe and socially sanctioned, open for all to see, or private and tense affairs with no necessary lasting damage, *or* a war literally to the death. Is it so?

● In *I'm OK – You're OK*, Thomas A. Harris sees transactional analysis as something that Teilhard de Chardin would have approved of – an opening to a future where the human race is free. This opening will be explored not by a nameless, corporate society but by individuals together in that society. The exploration can be made only as individuals are emancipated from the past and become free to choose either to accept or reject the values and methods of the past. One conclusion is unavoidable: Society cannot change until persons change.'

What do you think? Do individuals have that power? And how do people avoid turning the new freedom into another conforming institution?

● Dolph Sharp in 1974 wrote *I'm OK – You're Not So Hot – An*

Figure 16.

Impractical Guide to Transcendental Amnesia. In it his illustrator, Ed Powers, adapts the Yin–Yang diagram more or less as shown in Figure 16.

Sharp begins by saying he's not so hot, and asks how he fell into this deplorable state. Because of ambition, he says, because 'I had tried to better my Psychic Self' by reading how-to books. 'No sooner did a new Psych-Yourself-to-a-Happier-More-Productive-Sexier-Life book appear than I frantically bought it. Each evening at bedtime, I would mumble, "I'm OK, you're OK, she's OK, it's OK, we're OK, uncle Bill's OK" and so on.'

What state of mind were you in when you bought *this* book? What other kinds of books were on the shelf when you bought it? What label did the shelf have in the bookshop? And what does this say about you, me, and the rest of *Homo sapiens*?

● Would you describe yourself as 'eccentric'? If yes, why? If not, why not? Would you describe me as eccentric, based on the knowledge you have? If yes, why? If not, why not?

7

Centres of Self

'The remote village of Malana is well-known throughout Kulu,' wrote the anthropologist Colin Rosser in 1955. He was contributing a paper to a volume on the different kinds of villages to be found in India, their styles of organization and the ideas and attitudes among their inhabitants. The title of his paper, however, stressed the difference between Malana, a village in the Himalayas, and all the other villages and kinds of villages discussed in the book. Malana was known locally as the home of 'a different kind of people', so different that Rosser entitled the paper 'A Hermit Village'.

I do not know whether Malana is the same today as it was when Rosser undertook his field trip, nearly nine thousand feet up in 'a wild and isolated glen running roughly parallel to the Beas valley' under the 20,000-foot peak of Deo Tibba. I visited the region in the mid-1960s, travelling in local buses along the Beas valley. My wife and I found that valley isolated enough, and did not seek to cross the Chandrakanni Pass on foot to Malana. No doubt the region is just as isolated today, but that is hardly relevant. Rosser's point is timeless, concerning a community that has deliberately chosen to shun the rest of the world. For the 119 families of Malana the rest of the world was surplus to requirements.

When they met outsiders for the purpose of occasional trade, the people of the village would speak Kuluhi, the language of the area, but within the village they spoke Kanashi, 'which must be one of the smallest languages in the world', and a language basically different from Kuluhi. Inside the village community there were two castes, the dominant Kanets and three families of Lohars, effectively outcastes not just in the world at large but also in the tiny world of their village, where they lived off to one side, 'almost entirely ignored socially' though 'nonetheless indispensable from the economic and ritual points of view'.

For Rosser, the most interesting point about Malana was its religion. 'Throughout Kulu,' he notes, 'Malana is famed both for its village council and as "the village of Jamlu". Jamlu, the powerful tutelary deity of Malana, dominates and pervades the whole village. In his worship, the unity and solidarity of the village are strikingly and elaborately expressed. Jamlu is the ultimate authority, and the source of power, in the political, judicial, and religious spheres. In this sense, the god becomes something far more than a mere malevolent being whom it is as well to propitiate. To an important extent, Jamlu can be regarded as the deification of the village, and as the apotheosis of the villagers. His power and influence form an integral part of social control generally and of the political and judicial machinery in general.'

Already, in the strong technical description ('apotheosis of the villagers'; 'an integral part of social control'; 'the political and judicial machinery') we are forced beyond the picture of a remote little village of some 500 to 1,000 souls into thinking about the apparatus of larger and more convincing 'states' than little Malana. In the village, religious and secular authority do not just run together – they are one and the same, reminding one of the Old Testament Hebrews, of Cromwell's Puritans, of the structure of Mormonism, and other societies in which no line is or can be drawn between God's Covenant and human law. The council of Malana gains its authority from Jamlu and apart from it the Malanis are (or were) a remarkably egalitarian society – except, of course, for the low-caste Lohars. The council, which includes a number of elders, is run by three hierarchs: the *Karmisht* or Jamlu's manager, the *Pujara* or priest and the all-important *Gur* or mouthpiece of the god. The Karmisht is a chairman and treasurer, while true power lies with priest and mouthpiece, because together they express and interpret the will of Jamlu on earth.

How is this done? The *Gur* at certain ceremonies goes into a state of possession in which he becomes the vehicle of communication between the god and the villager. Shaking and trembling violently, with his uncut black hair swinging out as he shakes his head sharply from side to side to the sound of frenzied drumming by the band, he indeed looks like a wild figure. In this state he jerks out "with the voice of Jamlu" answers to questions put to him by devotees, directions about ceremonies, disputes, or problems troubling the village, and general harangues about the benefits of staunch belief, the necessity of following ancestral custom, and perhaps threats of what ill is likely to befall individuals or the village as a whole if the orders of the god are not obeyed.' The priest then reinforces his pronouncements.

Although there appears to be a remarkable degree of openness and public discussion within Malana this does not apply in Malana's relations with the outside world, or in cases of defiance of Jamlu's will. His automatic punishment of infringements is dire – by blindness, madness, leprosy, or death in really serious cases, and by inflicting a variety of lesser ills for minor deviations. All land in the area belongs to Jamlu, and the people see themselves as his tenants. Their fanaticism evokes in their neighbours a mixture of mockery and awe that is tinged with fear. They are perceived as an uncanny folk, best left alone. Rosser does not say how he managed to overcome their isolationism, but his remark that all who do not belong are treated with 'virulent suspicion and even contempt' must have applied in his case too. In that strange place, ostracism is one of the severest social sanctions available.

It must, at one and the same time, be both a great comfort and a great burden to be a tenant of Jamlu's.

At first sight it is a long way from Colin Rosser's account of the people of Malana to a book that was published a year later, in 1956, in Oxford. This was *A Historian's Approach to Religion*, by Arnold Toynbee, renowned as one of the few modern historians who have sought to see – and report upon – the human species as a whole. And yet it is not a long way at all, because this particular title reads like a scholarly expansion on the problem of Jamlu and his chosen people. Toynbee writes about the worship of nature and the possibility of Godhead, but his central concern is humankind's worship of itself and its own power, first of all as 'parochial communities', then as 'oecumenical communities and empires' (alongside the idolization of 'self-sufficient philosophers'). Two particular statements are worth highlighting:

The historian's point of view is not incompatible with the belief that

God has revealed Himself to Man for the purpose of helping Man to gain spiritual salvation that would be unattainable by Man's unaided efforts; but the historian will be suspicious, *a priori*, of any presentation of this thesis that goes on to assert that a *unique* and *final* revelation has been given by God to *my* people in *my* time on *my* satellite of *my* sun in *my* galaxy. In this self-centred application of the thesis that God reveals Himself to His creatures, the historian will espy the Devil's cloven hoof.'

'It is, in fact, difficult to imagine that a God whose mind and will govern the whole course of the Universe would compromise the conduct of His government by acting on a caprice. It would seem highly improbable that He would pick out just *me* and *my* tribe to be His prophet and His "Chosen People". Any such idea of mine would seem less likely to be the Truth than to be an hallucination conjured up by my innate self-centredness. And it would seem hardly more probable that God would choose out any other particular prophet or particular people to be the unique and final instrument of His purpose.'

And yet, as Toynbee himself demonstrates, this has been happening over and over again throughout recorded human history, and still happens around us with the creation of every new cult, sect, or other religious or quasi-religious outgrowth. Toynbee is not just questioning the Gurs and Pujaras of Jamlu but the major and minor prophets, messiahs, seers, gurus, god-men and man-gods of every time, place and persuasion, in so far as they have claimed (or it has been claimed for them) that they are God or the mouthpiece of God. No self-regarding group with any avatar or incarnation escapes, from Krishna of the *Bhagavad-Gita* to Joseph Smith among the Mormons, from Moses among the ancient Hebrews to Rajneesh and his sannyasins in Oregon, from Jesus Christ to Baha'u'llah, from Muhammad to L. Ron Hubbard and Scientology.

Some of us seek to respect all religions, and as many of their prophets and principles as possible. It is not easy. One difficulty is that when you meet the adherents of one particular system they are not always eager to return the respect. They may not even respect the respecter, returning deference with the kind of suspicion (and even contempt) that Rosser encountered in faraway Malana. In addition, when people like the historian Toynbee take the long view of humanity and its cultures it is fairly easy to be objective.

Most ideologies are distant in time and space and their deficiencies as a consequence easy to detect. Thus, the Hermopolitans with their fragments of the Great Egg Shell and the tenants of Jamlu afraid of his wrath are 'obviously' suffering under illusions. Jamlu, for example, in the view of some 99.999% of the human race, does not run the universe.

At the end of all conventional religious discussions the believers in X still insist that X is the truth while Y and Z are false – or simply not quite so true. At the same time the believers in Y or Z pat themselves on the back for being in the right camp, shaking their heads over the misguided foolishness of the Xites. At which point, if one seeks to be as objective as a Rosser or a Toynbee, it does look as though Jamlu, if not running the whole universe, is still doing rather well in running the human race – whatever name we give him.

What we are dealing with here is the business of closed societies, and the question of closed-off minds. My Glasgow Protestants and Catholics in the second chapter were in large part closed off from each other; the people of Malana are so organized as to seek separation from all of the rest of humanity, while my Urbanians simply operate institutions that create a certain mental set among many other mental sets (they get on quite well with their neighbours the Ruralians, but reckon them a rather backward lot). Using the Yin–Yang options it is clear that we can think of open and closed societies as distinct states (ours is open; Jamlu's is closed) or as a continuum (ours is more open than Jamlu's). But how does it all start and what perpetuates it?

The beginning of an answer can be found in words that Toynbee uses: 'this *self-centred* application of the thesis that God reveals Himself to His creatures' and 'an hallucination conjured up by my innate *self-centredness*'. Around the same time that Rosser and Toynbee were making their very different yet very similar reports to the rest of us, the psychoanalyst Erich Fromm was looking at the selfsame issue from yet another angle. In his *Psychoanalysis and Religion* in 1950 he developed the basic Freudian concern with incest towards the idea of the individual and the in-group: incest is more than physical sex with members of one's family; incest ties dating from birth create the dichotomy between the *familiar* – that is, 'what belongs to the family group' – and the *unfamiliar* – what is alien and 'out there'.

'Here', he says, 'are the roots of nationalism and racism, which in turn are the symptoms of man's inability to experience himself and others as free human beings.' It begins with the egocentric state of the small child, hardly aware of the separation of self from mother and environment. From total self-centredness the child moves out to being centred first in the immediate family, then in the clan or neighbourhood, then – if all goes well – in the larger community of religion and nation. The groupings to which man feels incestuously tied have become larger and the area of freedom has become greater, but the ties to those larger units which substitute for the clan and the soil are still powerful and strong. Only the complete eradication of the incest fixation will permit the realization of the brotherhood of man.'

One might rephrase that, as 'the realization of the unity of the human race', if one wished to avoid a male fixation in the use of the English language, a fixation that Toynbee and Fromm – along with many others of their generation – shared.

A year earlier than Fromm, in 1949, the cultural anthropologist Joseph Campbell published a work on mythology entitled *The Hero with a Thousand Faces*. Its purpose was, like Toynbee's and Fromm's, to talk universally about *Homo sapiens*, this time through the language and symbolism of many myths around the world that could be seen as just one myth, shared by all. Campbell was also concerned with the power of the infantile ego at work in our adult lives and with the projection of one's various in-groups onto the largest screen of all, the universe itself. He says:

Totem, tribal, racial, and aggressively missionizing cults represent only partial solutions of the psychological problem of subduing hate by love; they only partially initiate. Ego is not annihilated in them; rather, it is enlarged; instead of thinking only of himself, the individual becomes dedicated to the whole of *his* society. The rest of the world meanwhile (that is to say, by far the greater portion of mankind) is left outside the sphere of his sympathy and protection because outside the sphere of the protection of his god. And there takes place, then, that dramatic divorce of the two principles of love and hate which the pages of history so bountifully illustrate. Instead of clearing his own heart the zealot tries to clear the world. The laws of the City of God are applied only to his in-group (tribe, church, nation, class, or what not) while the fire of a perpetual holy war is hurled (with good conscience, and indeed a sense of pious service) against whatever

uncircumcised, barbarian, heathen, "native", or alien people happens
to occupy the position of neighbor. The world is full of the resultant
mutually contending bands: totem-, flag-, and party-worshipers.'

For Campbell 'the community today is the planet, not the
bounded nation' and 'the national idea, with the flag as totem, is
today an aggrandizer of the nursery ego, not the annihilator of
an infantile situation'. Like Fromm he favours a total escape from
such restrictions, with a conception of a God so all-inclusive that
in our awareness of such a deity we can 'then go forth as knowers
to whom all men are brothers'.

I chose this cluster of writers from around the early 1950s first
of all because they belong to that very period, not so long after
the end of a war in which ideologies figured most monstrously.
They were all conscious of the totalitarianism that precipitated the
Second World War, and, in the cases of Toynbee, Fromm and
Campbell, had a liberal and libertarian will to transcend the flag-
waving nationalisms and imperialisms that fed the conflagration.
I also chose them so that I could next ask: Do we remember them,
and have we built upon what they said, thirty years later? And,
thirdly, in terms of unitive thinking to ask: Is it enough and is it
practical, what Fromm and Campbell ask, that we extirpate utterly
the incest fixations that create such tribal gods as Jamlu?

I have been using various images from geometry to help me shape
and animate this book, and now I would like to return to the circle
image that I developed from Yin and Yang in the first chapter. This
time, however, I am less interested in the whole circle and its
perimeter shape than in the centre point of the circle. Toynbee talked
explicitly of a centre, using the words 'self-centred' and 'self-
centredness'. I added a little later the word 'egocentric', followed
by 'centred in the family' and so on. Now I'd like to look directly
at the idea of *centricity* itself, whether we link it to incest, religion,
or anything else.

We are all of necessity centric creatures, as the various writers
have indicated, in one way or another. To be born is to become
centric, and certainly, as Fromm argues, it is not difficult to imagine
a human being as something of a stone thrown into the pond of
the world, the first ripple of impact being *ego*centricity, the second
some kind of *ethno*centricity, and so on outward until the loyalty
and the joy of the liberated individual is the whole human
community across the planet.

Like the Piaget–Koplowitz stages in the preceding chapter, however, there is no guarantee that all human beings are equally capable in equal background conditions of reaching the great goal proposed by Fromm and Campbell of cosmopolitan unity. Again, as is so often the case, we have to imagine humanity strung out along an uneasy continuum from the awful security of Jamlu through smaller and larger loyalties to the greatest loyalty of them all (see Figure 17). And, I would add, we have to introduce a Maslovian element too. Just as, with Maslow's ladder of needs and their satisfaction, one can rise to greater heights then fall back in a crisis, so in this situation we might rise to great heights of non-incestuous internationalism, only to fall back again – in some ghastly crisis – into the abyss of ultranationalism or ego-absorption.

It is wonderful to propose shuffling off all the incest ties of the past, but it is not necessarily realistic to suppose that we can do this wholly and for ever. After all, in addition to the rational twin Verbella, we have in our brains the intuitive Pintorella, and then the edgy Horse and the snappy Crocodile. We have ideals, but we also have the baggage of everything else we are or ever have been.

Jamlu is part of us all, in one way or another. The tribal gods

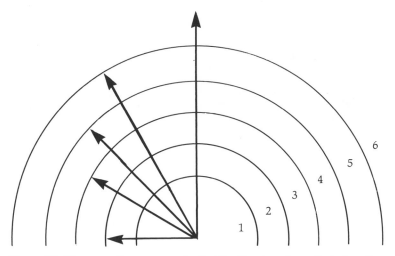

Figure 17. *The extending centres of self: (1) self as 'pure' ego (babyhood); (2) self and mother (infancy); (3) self and family (childhood); (4) self and nation, religion, language, gender, professionalism (etc); (5) self and all humanity; (6) self and the infinite.*

call to us, and threaten us with all sorts of plagues if we ignore them. We are born to different colours of skin, hair and eye, to different climates, living conditions and languages, to different educations into different religions, political ideologies, histories of race, nation and world, and finally into world-views whose limits we have never fully and consciously scanned. How, given that, can we hope to be holistic and cosmopolitan all of the time? The unitive answer – since it *is* unitive and not simply holistic – is that we have to live with all our fragments as best we can as well as with our glorious comprehensive dreams. The idea of integration presupposes a distintegrated state, a diversity that is not simply going to dissolve once we are 'whole'. With time it may all fit together more harmoniously, but the crises are always waiting to unsettle even the most stable and enlightened among us.

The unitive options, then, make allowance for the in-built disunities. In appropriate ways and at appropriate times one can enjoy a little egocentricity now and again ('Pamper yourself once in a while'), accept that one's ethnicity or one's background religion is a wonderful thing, despite the warts of history ('Here's tae us – wha's like us!', as I often say along with my fellow Scots, remembering all our own disunities too).

We are all centric creatures, but we also have in us the capacity to breach our centricities. It is on a range from hard to downright impossible to breach them totally, and move into a wholly different dimension of living, but we can breach them with greater or less success, for longer or shorter periods, and with this or that purpose in mind. It is also very likely that – being multiple creatures – we can have a variety of centres, and shift around from one to the other without becoming loaded down with guilt at our own hypocrisy and deviousness, looking over our shoulders to see whether Jamlu will visit leprosy upon us. As a simple example, take bilingualism. Someone who is competent in two languages may well also feel a slightly different person in each. I used to work in a French university in Canada, and when I was performing – especially for administrative purposes – in French I had a different body language, a differently shaped mouth, felt that I used my face differently, and even sometimes that I *thought* differently. This means that at the time I was sometimes Anglocentric and sometimes Francocentric – and this did not necessarily make me disloyal to anybody or anything.

The nineteenth-century Hindu sage Ramakrishna, the guru of the world-famous Swami Vivekananda, on the road to his enlightenment spent some time within the fold of the different major religions available to him in the Indian subcontinent. At one point he behaved as an orthodox Vaishnava or follower of Vishnu within Hinduism, at another time he was a Shaiva, or follower of Shiva. For a while he dressed and worshipped as a Muslim, then as a Christian. He did this, his followers in the Ramakrishna Mission assert, in order to try out the feel of the various creeds, and to demonstrate both their unity and his own spirit of inclusiveness. What the various Vaishnavas, Shaivas, Muslims and Christians who met him during this period thought about his transformations no one has recorded (as far as I know). Certainly he was a saintly figure known for this eccentricity. Many no doubt – then and now – would shrug and say that it was (possibly) a nice idea, but it was nonsense, because one *cannot* adopt and then discard the trappings and the teachings of one religion after another. They do not allow for it, and anyone who does it does not understand those religions or is a charlatan.

Maybe so, but I recall developing a Catholic cast of thought even in the short time that I spent in Pluscarden Priory as a young man, eager to escape my Glaswegian hate-reflex against Catholics. I recall even more strongly the insight into Greek Orthodox Christianity which I acquired in the short but important time I spent in the monasteries of Mount Athos in northern Greece. In India I visited and talked with many Hindu swamis and sadhus, and sought to understand their beliefs as much from the inside as a European could, and when my wife Feri and I met the Dalai Lama and other refugee Tibetans in Dharmashala – a hill station not all that far as the crow flies from Jamlu's Malana – we both felt a remarkable rapport with him and with the Tibetan monks as they debated and chanted and drank yak-butter tea. I often feel like a charlatan, but found those occasions to be times when I could breach the centricities of my own background without harm to myself or insult to my hosts.

It is, of course, a sort of eccentricity. But note the structure of the word. To be *eccentric* is to step outside the central area, to be a nonconformist in the eyes of the group that does the judging and uses the term. The prisoner in Plato's Cave who got up and 'saw the light' was clearly an outrageous eccentric to those who remained in their shackles. Anyone in Malana who defied Jamlu and left the village or talked about bringing in gadgets from the outside world would be a dangerous eccentric, meriting punishment. So it was once upon a time with Galileo Galilei and Giordano Bruno, in the eyes of the Roman Catholic Church; so it can be now with 'dissidents' in the Soviet Union who are 'heroes' in the eyes of many Americans. So it was until very recently with strong-minded vegetarians, so it still is with many feminists, who object to being bombarded all the time with phrases like 'the brotherhood of man'.

Artists are notorious eccentrics who are not always appreciated while alive. There is a very peculiar kind of eccentricity, too, if you like, among those who pay no attention to struggling artists under their noses while investing vast sums in a Picasso or a Van Gogh. If someone 'flashes' outside public lavatories in London, then that is eccentricity; it defies the norm. If someone advocates a worldwide Disaster Corps, to which national armies could contribute contingents, many might consider that rather eccentric, but much more usefully eccentric – if it could be achieved – than 'flashing', or increasing the money value of paintings by artists no longer able to benefit from the sale of their work.

On 18 June 1986 the *International Herald Tribune* published a report from Edinburgh, Scotland, by Richard F. Shepard. 'Here in Britain,' he wrote, 'where eccentricity has long been recognized as an established fringe of the social fabric, a scientific study of what it is all about is under way. The study, embracing 200 avowed eccentrics, is being conducted by Dr David Weeks, a former New Jersey resident who is principal psychologist of the Royal Edinburgh Hospital.' The project was then two years old and studied a variety of individuals: a man who had legally changed his name to Robin Hood, lived in Nottingham and wore Lincoln green; another, who lived in a cave, bare-foot and clad in pyjamas; others still who simply pursued bizarre schemes, often for the betterment of humanity.

Said Dr Weeks: 'They have an excessive preoccupation that they follow through on, and they don't care what others think. They are not hurtful. To the contrary, they are valuable to society, which is standardized and homogenized. International Computer, a large concern, was interested in the study because they wanted to send a letter designed to lure eccentrics, wild-idea people, to work for them.'

The study has already thrown up some characteristics of the eccentric personality. Eccentrics are often either only or eldest children, people who have received strict and critical parental supervision. They are not competitive, are loners rather than team players, do not have much of an urge to conform and often reckon that the world is out of step with *them*. They are obsessive, but often obsessively creative and inventive, as well as outspoken and opinionated. They may go through periods of low-profile 'invisibility', then burst forth on the world in a flamboyant fashion. And usually they are entirely aware of their differentness. The computer people, I suspect, were right in wanting to get in touch with them, as long as they also fully realized that 'wild-idea people' are in an important sense *wild* people. They are not, and choose not to be, domesticated by the norms of their society, and are therefore hard to live with.

The world of 'alternative lifestyles' is for many people an eccentric world, full of committed astrologers, vegetarians, reincarnationists, Aquarian Agers, yogis and Zen Buddhists, biorhythmicians, Ginseng-takers, Tarot specialists, UFO enthusiasts, and Ouija board practitioners who may well talk to their plants and keep a black cat. The Hippie Revolution in North America, coinciding as it did with major political and social issues like the Vietnam War and accompanied by drugs and the long trail to Kathmandu, promoted eccentricity on a quite massive scale – and ultimately produced its own conformities, its own badges and uniforms.

Such wholesale movements and individual efforts at breaching one circle or another, however, have their cumulative effect, and there are many things in the world today – from forms of language to fashion, from attitudes to activities – that are strongly established inside the circles of our daily lives because of what went on in the 1960s and still goes on in alternative enclaves. If a middle-class housewife is 'uptight', she might well get a leotard and go to a yoga class – and start reading odd-ball books about things like unitive thinking. Imagine her mother doing that during the years when Fromm, Toynbee and Campbell were hoping for a wiser and more open world.

Follow-up to Chapter 7

● You may or may not have visited India. If you have visited India

you may or may not have visited Himachal Pradesh. If you have
visited Himachal Pradesh you may or may not have reached Kulu.
If you have reached Kulu, it is highly unlikely that you were inclined
to cross the Chandrakanni Pass to visit Malana. But you may well
have met Jamlu the jealous god somewhere else. Where was that?

● Here is a quotation from another of Arnold Toynbee's works,
Mankind and Mother Earth (1976):

> The biosphere is a film of dry land, water, and air enveloping the globe
> (or virtual globe) of our planet Earth. It is the sole present habitat –
> and, as far as we can foresee today, also the sole habitat that will ever
> be accessible – for all the species of living beings, including mankind,
> that are known to us.'

Consider this quotation from the following points of view:

○ the kluuls from Arcturus, circling the Earth in their invisible
starship
○ the Urbanians, with their preferences for rectangular shapes
○ the people of Malana, whose interest does not extend beyond
the land they rent from their god Jamlu
○ militant feminism
○ the concept of centricity as outlined in this chapter

● The following is from Irma Kurtz, *Malespeak*, 1986:

> The human male is an orthodox creature, conventional in his tastes
> . . . When a male dares to be unconventional he makes a go of it only
> if other men follow him, incidentally attracting women to the camp
> of, say, Marxism, Calvinism, Freudianism, Mohammedanism, or good
> old Christianity. It is not equally difficult for a woman to be
> unconventional with impunity because she is a smaller threat to the
> status quo . . . Inside my own family, for instance, as inside bigger
> society, it was easier for me to accomplish a personal rebellion . . .
> than it would have been for my brother-the-doctor . . . When a man
> is courageous enough to become an eccentric, a rebel, an artist, he stands
> to be one of the most magnificent successes in human history precisely
> because the odds are so much against him.'

Is this so? Is the price of eccentricity – in the community you know
– different for men and for women?

● Great yogis and swamis are supposed to be detached. Here is a quotation from Swami Sivananda of Rishikesh, from the booklet *Light on Culture*, circulated in the early 1960s:

> 'Glory to India who has preserved in her bosom the message of dharma, renunciation, selfless service and universal love. India will not be able to rival the West in physical science but in the spiritual field she will certainly be unparalleled . . . The main glory of India is in her rishis and seers . . . The Hindu religion had attained a very high status in arts, philosophy, morality and culture long before any other religion was born.'

How do you respond to this statement, made by one of the most influential yogis of this century? Do you accept it as true, or as something else? If something else, how might it fit into the concept of centricity? If it fits, what does that prove, if anything?

● Imagine that my kluuls from Arcturus make themselves known to you, much in the way that UFO 'aliens' reportedly contact us now and again. Suppose that they offer you a trip back to Arcturus with them, assuring you that you would be able to return again to Earth. Would you go? If you would, why? If you wouldn't, why?

8

The Scale of Things

In *Gulliver's Travels*, first published in 1726, Jonathan Swift sent his hero first to the land of Lilliput, then to the land of Brobdingnag. Among the Lilliputians he was 'the Man Mountain', while among the Brobdingnagians he was something of a toy.

Or, as the astronomer Frank H. Shu put it, in *The Physical Universe* in 1982: 'The primary inhabitants of the universe are stars, of which the Sun is only one example. Stars exhibit a great variety of properties. Besides suns of all colors, there are the tremendously distended *red giants* and the mysteriously tiny *white dwarfs*. The Sun itself is quite an average star, neither very massive nor very light, neither very large nor very small. Why, then, does the Sun appear so bright, but the stars so faint? Because the stars are much further away than the Sun. The Sun is "only" eight light-minutes away, but the nearest star, proxima Centauri, is about four light-years distant.'

To astronomers at large our sun is classified as a *yellow dwarf*: Capella is ten times bigger, Antares is 300 times bigger, and some of the *supergiants* are 3,000 times bigger. Such statements appear to be cosmic facts, to be accepted by the ignorant majority of us without argument. But like light-minutes and light-years, such facts are hard to digest – hard even to bring into the mind. Or as Robin Kerrod in *The Universe*, published in 1975, has put it: 'It is difficult for anyone, even astronomers included, to view the universe in perspective. We know that it is made up of space with stars, planets, dust, and gas floating in it here and there. But empty space predominates'.

Kerrod adds that the solar system in which we live, move and have our being is in fact 'a relatively crowded corner of the universe', something that from our everyday point of view is hard to credit. By our standard methods of measuring distances the planet Venus, a nearer neighbour, is more than 25 million miles or 40 million kilometres away, while the sun that lights our days is 93 million miles or 150 million kilometres away. It is quite hard enough to imagine these distances; more difficult still when astronomers tell us that they are examples of interstellar crowding and a mere nothing anyway on the cosmic scale of things.

Today, most people with a Western-style education accept that the universe is enormous beyond conception, yet we do not obtain this information and awareness from our normal sense impressions, which are not equipped to register it. This is the reason for the very difficulty we have in grasping such things. Whatever conception we do have of the vastness of things is mediated by the intellect, not the senses: we cannot 'see' the universe spread out with all its turning galaxies – the sun does not look like a twinkling star – we do not feel the earth moving on its axis or in its orbit round the sun, and certainly not in its passage across the galaxy along with the sun. On the contrary, our sensory evidence runs the other way: the earth seems to stand still while everything else moves round it, and except when ships descend out of sight over the horizon or when we are high in the atmosphere in an aircraft we remain flat-earthists every one. This is the practical, everyday 'reality' that science rejects as the *geo*centric view of things. Science has even rejected the *helio*centric view of things that once looked so radical. If there is any centre to the universe, so scientists speculate, it is far away from us and probably consists of a black hole, another construct that is deeply hard to fathom.

People with a contemporary-style education can be said, as a consequence of all this, to have a dual system of knowledge and awareness: a science-based appreciation of how things are, and a practical everyday knowledge of sunrises and sunsets when the sun neither rises nor sets. In the first, we are micro-Lilliputians; in the second we have *some* size and substance.

Let us, however, push the scientific scale as far as it will go. First, the macrocosm, the infinity above and beyond us. Says Robin Kerrod, imagine a sphere of space that encompasses the whole planet Earth and is about 15,000 miles (24,000 km) across. That

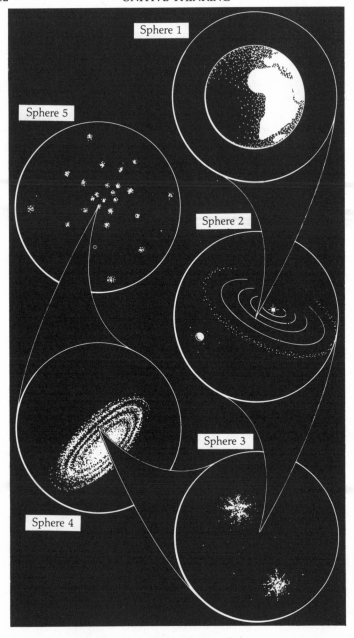

Figure 18. *The multiplied spheres of the macrocosm.*

already makes each one of us and all our dreams extremely small. Now multiply that sphere 40,000 times. The diameter of the new sphere would be equal to the radius – just the radius – of the orbit of the planet Jupiter round the sun. Multiply that second sphere another 40,000 times and we get a third sphere; if our entire solar system were on the surface of one side of *that* sphere, the nearest star, proxima Centauri, would be on the surface directly opposite. Now multiply another 40,000 times, and we get a fourth sphere large enough to hold all of the one galaxy that contains our solar system. Then multiply another 40,000 times to get a fifth sphere that holds about a third of the known universe. (See also Figure 18.)

The mind staggers in the effort to grasp such sizes, even with the help of illustrations. That, all astronomers agree, is a fair representation of the macrocosm, the vastness onto which we project our images of both the gods and God, where angels and demons once wrestled for our souls (and for many people still wrestle for our souls) in the heavens and hells of our imagining. In the face of such vastness even God shrinks – or grows so large that it is hard to conceive Him, Her, It or Them ever giving a hyperthought for microcosmic us.

But there is also the microcosm, the infinity below and within us. In *Atoms and Energy*, also published in 1975, and like Kerrod's work aimed at the younger reader, Neil Ardley offers some analogies to help us 'see' just how small 'small' can be. He says: 'The atom is unbelievably small. It is so small that if a car were enlarged to the size of the sun, one of its sparking plugs would be the size of the earth.' If that were so, a single molecule in the metal of the sparking plug would be about the size of the city of Paris, while one atom inside that molecule would have the dimensions of a dinner plate – and the nucleus of that atom would be no larger than a pin-prick. (See also Figure 19.)

Theoretical physicists more than anyone else live their professional lives in a mental universe where these scales are 'real', and can be interpreted and expressed with mathematical elegance. Whether or not they spend much time considering the sheer quantity of 'empty' space at both the macrocosmic and the microcosmic levels I do not know. But the sheer potency of their mysterious craft – for good and for ill – is exhibited for us every day in the technologies that use electricity and magnetism, nuclear energy and fibre optics. Their theories of what the universe is

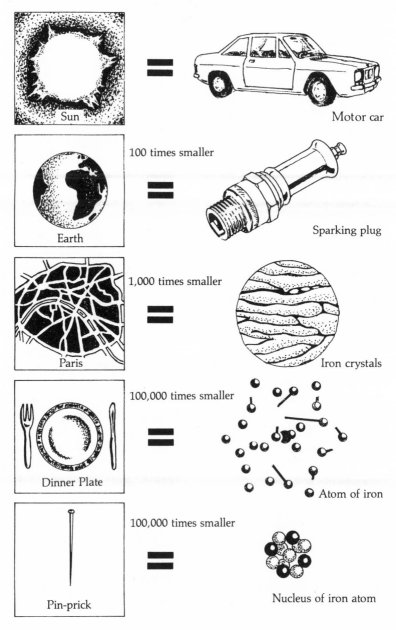

Figure 19. *The diminishing spheres of the microcosm.*

(including how vast it is above and below, within and beyond us) are so practical in their effects that they must give even the most antiscientific among us moments of deep awe and appreciation.

On one occasion I was chatting to a friend and academic colleague, Jean-Paul de Chezet, about all this. As linguists we were both concerned not just with the 'reality' of these scientific scales but also with whether language could cope in the business of discussing and describing them. 'I suppose we live in the mesocosm,' he said.

The mesocosm. It's a nice idea. We are creatures of the middle point, born into consciousness at the level where the dance of nature – particles in atoms, atoms in molecules, molecules in substances, substances in suns and worlds, suns and worlds in galaxies, galaxies in a cosmos with no perceivable limit – where that dance translates to our senses the planetary conditions that provide not just 'life' but also 'meaning'. And if we ever met the kluuls we would need to translate our meaning into theirs and back again, never quite succeeding, just as we never quite succeed in translating even English into French or French into English.

Add the dimension of time. Our home planet is wrapped in a blanket of gases that encompass it in several layers, and the world is itself like an onion, structured in concentric shells outward from its core. The blanket of gases – the atmosphere – flows in winds, while the seas move in currents. The ground beneath us, however, appears solid and unchanging, until we add the dimension of time. Geologists assure us that continents are not truly stable. They too move and have their currents. The land north and north-east of the Great Lakes in North America is slowly rising; docks for ships, built many years ago, are now high above water level. Columns that support an ancient temple near Naples in Italy have holes bored in them – by sea animals. Clearly, the temple was submerged and rose again from the sea by natural processes over which you and I have no control whatsoever – and of which, without science, we would have little worthwhile awareness.

The liquids of the sea and the gases of the air move at speeds and in ways that we understand and accept, but the changes in the 'solid' earth beneath us suggest that, on a time-scale commensurate with macroscosmic and microcosmic scales of size, there are great slow currents in operation inside the onion-like layers that make up the planet. Some scientists maintain that heat deep inside our planet–spaceship causes materials to expand and move upwards, cooling down as they approach the surface. In cooling, these materials settle down once more, but in the process of doing so disturb the thin crust above them – the crust that we regard as solid rock. Such a resettling is the merest twitch of the skin for Mother Earth, but for us the result might be the devastation that visited, for example, Southern Italy in 1980, destroying the homes of tens of thousands of people.

In the mesocosm, our situation is inherently a paradox. On our own scales of size and worth we have mighty cities and ancient cultures; in cosmic terms, we are – as Arthur Conan Doyle once suggested in his story *When the World Screamed* – 'tiny animalcules' that have collected on the surface of the planet during its travels round the sun 'as barnacles gather on an ancient vessel'. Depending on the scale used, we are either nature's greatest achievement – or a parasitic growth.

We live on our earthship within very strict limits indeed, within what since the start of this century scientists and thinkers have been calling the 'biosphere'. As Arnold Toynbee has said, 'In terrestrial terms the biosphere is fantastically thin. Its upper limits may be equated with the maximum altitude in the stratosphere at which a plane can remain air-borne; its lower limits is the depth, below the surface of its solid portion, to which engineers can mine and bore. The thickness of the biosphere, between these two limts, is minute by comparison with the length and radius of the globe which it coats like a delicate skin.'

Within these limits, on this fragile stage, all the dramas of human history have been performed: all the designs like Yin and Yang have been created, all the theories like Tantra have been woven, all the fables and parables told.

There are some billions of us swarming with the other myriads of earthly life-forms around the biosphere of Old Mother Earth – some being constructive, others being destructive, others just being, and few of us entirely sure what constructive and destructive mean in the long term. Each one of those millions of us consists of billions of living and dying cells, the whole complex supervised by a brain and a nervous system that has in excess of 10 billion neurons or nerve cells helping to run the show – a show that never stops, even when we are engaged in what tradition tells us is 'sleep'.

Perhaps a few thousand years ago things were a little easier conceptually. Nobody knew any of the statistics I have brought together in this chapter. Pictures of how the world worked were essentially 'mythological', a term that is often used to suggest inferiority in the face of science. In creative terms there is nothing at all inferior about the many mythologies bred by the curiosity and narrative skills of *Homo sapiens*, and scientific theory today is no more and no less than a traceable outgrowth from such tales and descriptions. Some systems like the traditional Christian one saw the cosmos as relatively small, and measured the history of the race in a line from Creation through Fall to Redemption to Second Coming and Judgement – only a few thousand years for the whole drama. Others, like Hinduism, have envisaged aeons of time not unlike those of the geologists and vast spaces similar to those of the astronomers, but in terms of a great wheel turning, turning, changing, changing, with all of us on it. And our minds and brains have been fed bits of this system and bits of that, with an overlay of modern science – creating among the billions of brain cells the individual crazy codes that make us unique and give us our private understandings and confusions.

There is a cliché for all of this, just as there are clichés for most of the important things of life. Like most clichés it has been used so often that its sparkle has vanished away, but that does not affect its core of appropriateness, which is quite simply that truth *is* stranger than fiction – and, by extension, that fiction is only strange because it has the weird and wonderful mesocosm to draw on for inspiration.

Curiously enough, we all know this. I haven't said anything at all in this chapter which is not easily accessible information. In a broad sense most people with books, newspapers, radios and televisions at their elbows know the things that I have been describing – or could look them up in some repository of information. The very relativity of it all is represented in one of the most familiar of all clichés – the response, 'Well, it depends', when someone is asked a question that can only be answered by finding or constructing a context in which that question makes sense. If there is no context – no appropriate region of macrocosm, mesocosm or microcosm – there is no answer.

In Zen Buddhism it is asserted that we already know everything we need to know in order to manage, to cope with existence – to be free. There is a story that one day Gensha was meditating and heard the voice of a swallow.

'Ah,' he said, 'how well that swallow has explained both the nature of things and the truth of the Lord Buddha.'

He then came down from his seat, and a little later one of the other monks, eager for clarity, went to Gensha and said, 'I didn't understand what you meant when you were talking about the swallow.'

'Go away then!' answered the master. 'How can anyone possibly trust you?'

The implication of tales like these, says R. H. Blyth, is that all questioning of other people in order to get their help is a way of avoiding the real answer. We are all enlightened, say the Zen masters, but wish that we were not. We all know what and where we are, that we should take care of each other better, that life is both dark and bright, that we are all both important and unimportant, that everything depends on everything else, and that contexts change the ways in which problems can be solved. We all hear the same swallow, but the interpretation – or lack of interpretation – that we place on its song is ours alone. If we know all of this and still prefer the mantle of ignorance, says Gensha, then we are evasive and hypocritical – and how can we be trusted?

It is a sobering thought, as Gensha meant it to be for the novice monk. It suggests, as both neurologists and psychologists also tell us, that generally we hear what we want to hear and see what we want to see. We are certainly selective creatures and could not manage in a world of sense impressions if we were not. But how we go about the selection is crucial.

I mentioned 'meaning' a little earlier, when talking about the dance of the atoms and the stars. As we grow up from the egocentric state of the child we suppose that there is a fixed meaning out there and that we grow up into understanding it. Our social conditioning reinforces this idea, because it can make a lot of sense – in survival terms and as regards group cohesion against the outside world – for everybody in a culture and a community to 'see' the world the same way. It is only when we find ourselves in Marshall McLuhan's global village on the edge of nuclear or ecological catastrophe that the benefit of a more inclusive kind of 'seeing' becomes obvious. There was nothing obvious about it in the past and for many people within the citadels of tradition there is nothing obvious about it even now. The idea that there *is* a fixed meaning out there is still

strong, and possesses the minds of all of us either some of the time
or most of the time. I doubt that it possesses all of our minds all
of the time. There are, I suspect, for everybody moments of unitive
experience – cool and at the same time awesome – in which Jamlu's
will becomes puny and limited, even to Jamlu's greatest defenders.

There may be all kinds of higher significance out there in the
cosmos. Such significance, however, is on a scale and at a level
of presentation that are beyond the capacity of our psycho-physical
apparatus to handle. If it is there then it is at a 'divine' level, not
accessible to us in its totality. Even those religious movements which
insist that God has revealed His Truth to humankind on one or
more occasions agree that the 'revelation' is not ultimate but occurs
in terms of our capacity to receive it. It has therefore been rendered
mesocosmic, scaled down, or diluted. The undiluted message, like
the unshielded light from the Burning Bush, would be too strong
for the human receiver, however well tuned – and would destroy
it. The 'truth' of God is therefore less than the truth of God.

It is an attractive picture, suggesting both concern and
compassion on the part of the awesome power in the heart of suns
and galaxies. For the religious it is reassuring, but for the non-
religious it may be no more than poetry, and rather pathetic poetry
at that, because for them the power in the heart of suns and galaxies
is not so contrived as to 'feel' or 'do' anything anthropomorphic
at all: we are not made in its image nor it in ours; it contains us,
but it does not cuddle us – ever. So, if there *is* a higher order of
truth out there and it did make itself available in a reduced
mesocosmic way to us, we would still argue about it and might
not be that much further forward at the end of the day. One might
suppose that an all-knowing deity, having made us the way that
we are in a world like this one, might find (or have found long
ago) a better way of handling such wayward midgets.

So, whether or not that higher-order truth *is* out there, we –
as we grow up and as the species evolves – are left not so much
taking meaning from the universe as offering meaning to it.

Take the statistics of science that we looked at earlier. They have
come into existence through our extending our limited senses with
the help of telescopes and mathematical models, and the scales of
size to help us understand both galaxy and atom are of our own
making. Nobody gave us those scales. Jupiter does not know that
it belongs in a sphere 40,000 times larger than one that just contains

the earth; molecules do not know that they would be the size of the city of Paris if the car of which they are part were as large as the sun. These scales are pictures – parables again – that have subjective validity for us, struggling to understand, but no objective worth for the universe at large. They are all mesocosmic constructs – or, in simpler terms, arrangements to make our minds more comfortable. They leave the cosmos untouched, except for the important human point that we have projected a meaning outwards that was not there for us before.

The idea that meaning is given and not taken has profound implications. It is not only compatible with much of modern science but is also part and parcel of much mystical philosophy. Fritzhof Capra has pointed this out in his *Tao of Physics* (1975), where he argued that quantum mechanics and oriental mysticism are discussing the same ultimates. It is not surprising that many people, both physicists and traditional religionists, are unwilling to think like that – they do not want to know. But the idea is revolutionary, not just in suggesting that science and mysticism can meet but also in implying that humanity may one day have a unified meaning to project outward into the cosmos. To date we have had a wild array of conflicting meanings, and I am always a little suspicious of 'one' way of looking at anything (because the one way is usually conducive to one kind of fascism or another). Better, perhaps, to suggest that we could have a sufficiently unitive species-wide way of seeing our predicament so that all the weird and wonderful pictures that we have ever had could be put in perspective and made available as needed to enrich our understanding of life.

As things stand, our general understanding of life and the universe in which we are embedded splits into two modes of thinking and feeling: a Yin of materialism versus a Yang of spiritualism. That is, we seek to account for things either in terms of matter alone, everything reduced to units of various kinds operating together according to natural 'laws' – or we seek to account for things in terms of spirit working upon matter (usually at the behest of deity), in which one can expand out of the immediately material into endless worlds or planes of otherness, where the true purposes of existence are to be understood. These are the polarities. Many of us cleave to one pole rather than another, many of us make compromises between the poles (as for example a scientist who pursues during work-days the materialist, reductionist model, then on Sunday goes to church), while many more slide back and forth depending upon circumstances, social pressures and the company we keep. Conventionally, there are no other options available.

Unconventionally, however, and in unitive terms, there *are* other options. The previous paragraph can be handled fairly well by means of the three options of the split-circle diagram (as in Chapter 1). You can then have Option 1, which is either materialism or spiritualism, and never the twain shall meet. Or you can have Option 2, where there are both materialism and spiritualism as a kind of continuum, and you can locate yourself where you please. Option 3 accepts that at times the division is sharp as in Option 1 and at times fuzzy as in Option 2 – and one operates accordingly.

Suppose, however, that we really *do* impose our meanings on the world around us – individually and collectively – rather than receiving those meanings as the data of life. Suppose also that the three options above will always apply, because the poles of materialism and spiritualism have both been with us a long time and may well be inherent in how as a species we think, feel and behave. *Then* suppose that neither has ultimate merit, because both are the products of limited minds with limited experience using the limited codes called human language and symbolism. Suppose, that is, that by their very nature neither of the views on its own can possibly have got it right. Let's look squarely at how they have both changed in their histories – look at all the forms of spiritual disagreement in all the religions of the world, and how materialism has, among other things, moved from the clockwork imagery of Newton to the space–time continuum of Einstein and the uncertainty principle of Heisenberg.

All of them, both of the great polarities – these are all hypotheses, all models, all *crutches* to help us limp along our mesocosmic road. None is anywhere near comprehensive enough to cover what we are and where we are, not the many gods of Hinduism, not the one God of Judaism and Islam, not the three-in-one God of Christianity, not the atman and Brahman of Indian philosophy, not the idea of spirit nor the idea of matter, not the theory of evolution nor the essence of quantum mechanics. Some are better than others, some are better than others for some things, but none excels because none *can* excel – certainly not while we are as we currently are. All, however, are fine artifacts if we accept their strengths and weaknesses. All are tools, ready to hand, available for application to problems, available for synthesis or separation, available as part of the broad legacy of the race, without fear or favour.

Follow-up to Chapter 8

● Usually people talk about 'the universe', and much less commonly 'a universe'. Here, however, is a quotation from Edward R. Harrison's *Cosmology: The Science of the Universe*, published by Cambridge University Press in 1981 (the writer is both a physicist and an astronomer):

> The history of cosmology shows us that in every age devout people believe that they have at last discovered the true nature of the Universe, whereas in each case they have devised a world picture – merely a universe – that is like a mask fitted on the face of the still unknown Universe . . . Because we do not know, and in our wildest dreams cannot imagine, the true nature of the Universe, we may avoid referring to it directly by using the more modest word *universe*. A universe is simply a model of the Universe.'

To this he adds the following diagram, with the caption: 'The Universe contains us, the cosmologists, who construct the many universes.'

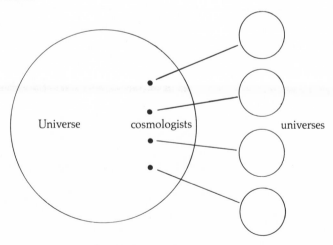

Have you ever met a cosmologist? Would you recognize one if you did?

● In his book, Edward Harrison discusses the old geocentric and heliocentric models of the universe, then talks about 'the twentieth-century isotropic universe in which all directions are observed to be alike'. In contrast, the *Rig-Veda* of the ancient Hindus, over three thousand years ago, talked about our familiar idea of a universe with up, down and sideways in it. But even there one finds remarkable freedom of thought:

> In the beginning was darkness wrapped in darkness
> And everything was unmanifest water;
> Whatever was, that Unity, coming into being, hidden by
>   the void,
> Was kindled through the power of heat . . .

> In the beginning this Oneness evolved . . .
> Was there a below? Was there an above?
> Scatterers of seed there were, and powers,
> With energy beneath and impulse above.

> Who knows truly? Who can here declare it?
> Whence was it born, whence came this emanation?
> By its coming forth the gods came into being
> But who knows where it came from?

> Where this emanation came from –
> Whether a god created it, or whether he didn't;
> Only its overseer in the highest heaven knows –
> Or perhaps he does not know either.

● 'Who are the cosmologists?' Harrison asks. 'Professional cosmologists are relatively few in number; they are well versed in mathematics, physics, and astronomy, and they study the large-scale structure of the physical universe. Everybody else is occasionally an amateur cosmologist. When somebody stands back from the study of a specialized area of the sciences or humanities and reflects on things in general, and tries to see the forest and not just the trees, tries to see the whole picture and not just the dabs of paint, the whole tapestry and not the threads, that person becomes a cosmologist.'

● The story goes that after a lecture on cosmology that included the nature of the solar system, the philosopher William James was confronted by a little old lady who told him that he had got it all wrong.

'My theory is better,' she said.

'And what is your theory, Madam?' he asked politely.

'Well, we live on a crust of earth that is on the back of a giant turtle.'

'And what does the turtle stand on?' asked James.

'You're a clever man, Mr James, and that's a good question, but the answer to it is that the first turtle stands on the back of a second even larger turtle, directly underneath.'

'And the second turtle – what does it stand on?' asked James patiently.

'Aha, it's no use arguing, Mr James. You see, it's turtles all the way down.'

Have you ever met that little old lady?

● Going by what you have read so far, is 'unitive thinking' just mysticism under another name, is it really ancient or is it a modern mix of various philosophies of life? Is it 'thinking' at all in the proper sense of the word, or is it more a matter of attitude(s)?

9

Vertical, Lateral and Unitive

The large bird, a heron, is patrolling the water's edge, scanning for fish. In its beak it is holding a small feather, and at just the right moment it drops the feather gently into the stream. A small fish rises to the lure and the heron strikes.

Is it instinct, entirely, that governs the action of this bird, or is it intelligence? Is the heron, in any sense that we can relate to, *thinking* about what it is doing?

By and large it has been the view of educated people in the West for some hundreds of years that animals are a kind of robot life, conditioned through the programs of their nature — whether at the will of God or through evolutionary development – to behave in certain ways and to be unable to amend those ways from situation to situation in ways that we – the supreme animal – would accept as conscious and intentional. Says the biologist Donald R. Griffin in *Animal Awareness*, published in 1981:

> The possibility that animals have mental experiences is often dismissed as anthropomorphic because it is held to imply that other species have the same mental experiences a man might have under comparable circumstances. But this widespread view itself contains the questionable assumption that human mental experiences are the only kind that can conceivably exist. This belief that mental experiences are a unique attribute of a single species is not only unparsimonious; it is conceited. It seems more likely than not that mental experiences, like many other characters, are widespread, at least among multicellular animals, but differ greatly in nature and complexity.'

The ethologist James L. Gould has tended to believe that most animal behaviour is of the pre-wired variety, holding the view that evolution is capable of programming very complex behaviour into very limited brain space – as for example the heron, with a brain less than a tenth the size of ours. Gould's area of research, however, has concerned creatures with even tinier brains – the honey-bees. These insects are capable of extremely complex dances that serve to help foragers locate food in relation to the sun's position in the sky even on partly cloudy days. At a conference in Washington in the early 1980s – as reported by Bayard Webster in the *New York Times* (June 1983) – Gould somewhat ruefully described a recent experiment that he had carried out.

He observed bees as they flew to a food source that he had located with care at sites which were regularly moved farther and farther from the hive. Whenever they were moved, the distance was increased by a factor of 1.25 – one and a quarter times the distance of the previous location. To his considerable surprise he discovered that the foraging honey-bees were predicting where the next food source would be. When he reached his next carefully plotted site, often hundreds of metres from the hive, there the bees would be circling the likely spot. At the conference he was asked to explain how these little creatures could manage such a trick.

'I can't explain it,' he said. 'I wish they'd never done it.'

Ethologists and other investigators of animals now have such a range of more-than-instinctive patterns in their data that the idea of our own cognitive uniqueness is beginning to crumble a bit at the edges. What we appear to be witnessing here is the shift from a simple container model (with 'humans can think' in one container, and 'animals can't think' in the other) to a continuum model (in which all living creatures are located along a complex continuum of less to more, with 'different' featuring heavily along the way). It only surprises me that, since evolution is such a powerful explanatory theory and rests on the idea called 'gradualism', it has taken so long to switch to a richer and more useful model.

Such a model would then have to assume, not unreasonably, that our remote ancestors – in a mix of nature and nurture – became capable of a greater capacity to think as their brains achieved the size and diversity discussed in Chapter 5. As survival devices, large human brains justify their existence only to the extent that they help us solve at our level more complex problems on a day to day basis than the honey-bees and the herons solve in their quest for food. Whatever else *they* may have 'in mind' besides food, we have the Maslovian ladder of needs, and much of our thinking relates to such needs. As Edward de Bono has put it, in *Practical Thinking* (1971):

> 'Everyday thinking is what fills in the time when you are neither asleep nor dead. Just as you notice a car engine only when it is not running smoothly so you become aware of everyday thinking when it is not running smoothly. Everyday thinking is involved in family squabbles; making mayonnaise; planning a holiday; what to do about the dog when you want to go away for the week-end; thinking of an excuse for getting to work late; finding an easy way of getting through your work; educating the children; opening a bottle of beer when you have lost the opener; keeping your end up in a political argument; and possibly trying to make the world a better place to live in.'

Homo sapiens has been engaging in this kind of massive, half-conscious, casual but purposeful mentation for millennia. It was only comparatively recently – as far as we can tell from the records, only about 2,500 years ago – that intellectuals began to think about thinking; when they began to do this, they also began to systematize it, and it is intriguing that the systematizing of thought began at precisely the time when people like Gautama the Buddha were systematizing 'paths' and 'ladders' to what they saw as better lives, in or beyond this world. Even the Buddha, concerned with a massive and shape-free sunburst of 'enlightenment', set out to lead others towards it *systematically* – by making lists of dos and don'ts and classifying both the world and one's responses to it (as in Figure 15, Chapter 6).

The two major areas where thinking about thinking took place – changing civilization in the process – were ancient Greece and India. In both places the philosophers who venerated orderly thought emerged from matrices of religion and mysticism: in Greece, from the sect of the Pythagoreans, who venerated numbers, speculated about geometric shapes, and believed in reincarnation; in India among the brahmins, who were inordinately fond of classifying, also venerated numbers, and also believed in reincarnation. In Greece it took many hundreds of years before their schools of thought coalsced under the one word 'logic' – coined by Alexander of Aphrodisias in the second century AD – but the processes of linear thinking were vigorously pursued by Socrates, Plato, Aristotle and others within such frameworks as rhetoric, philosophy and grammar, and make the foundation of much of what centrally passes for 'thought' in Western education today. In India a major school coalesced earlier, the classical system known as Nyaya, which is hardly known outside India today, but was in its time at least as rich and influential as the Greek tradition.

Both systems used organized thought as a tool – indeed, Aristotle's great work on the subject is the *Organon*, a name that underlies the world 'organize' and translates as 'tool' or 'instrument'. The significant difference between classical Greek and Hindu rationalism, however, was that where Western formal reasoning has taken seriously only the complementary processes called deduction and induction, the Hindu logic of Nyaya allows for four kinds of perception to which thought is necessarily linked: sense perception, mental perception, self-consciousness, and yogic intuition. Where the Greeks and their legatees have assumed only one mind equipped with senses and the ability to reflect, the Hindus have assumed as given four coequal awarenesses: through the body, through the mind, through the higher consciousness of self, and from a source beyond the phenomenal world of Maya. It is only in the last two centuries – and increasingly in the last two or three decades – that this other model of perception and thought has become available for Westerners to study and make use of.

In the meantime, the West has raised the linear style of Greek logic into supreme position. So successfully has this been done that it appears to be a universal state of affairs. It has led Edward de Bono to observe (in *The Use of Lateral Thinking*, 1967), that 'vertical thinking has always been the only respectable type of thinking. In its ultimate form as logic it is the recommended ideal towards which all minds are urged to strive, no matter how far short they fall. Computers are perhaps the best example. The problem is defined by the programmer, who also indicates the path along which the problem is to be explored. The computer then proceeds with its uncomparable [*sic*] logic and efficiency to work out the problem. The smooth progression of vertical thinking, from one solid step to another solid step is quite different from lateral thinking.'

The contrast between the 'vertical' and the 'lateral' – a metaphor of spatial distribution – gives us a powerful picture of what de Bono sees. We have a container model here (to use another metaphor), in that there is a choice between one style of thinking and another: either the Yin of Verticality or the Yang of Laterality. You may climb the ladder of logic rung by rung, or you may jump off that ladder into some other area. The only reason for making the jump, however, is to find a link between the first area of thinking and a new area, in order to solve a problem in a strikingly new, creative and effective way. This is parabolic or analogic reasoning, as discussed in Chapter 4 – recognized as legitimate by the Greeks and Hindus both consciously as well as in their liberal use of comparisons, analogies, metaphors and parables. And, indeed, it is reassuring and galvanizing to find that the ancient non-linear devices of the paradox and the parable are potent – though often inexplicit – tools in de Bono's powerful new models of practical thought.

Foremost among them is what one might call the Parable of the Pebbles, with which *The Use of Lateral Thinking* begins. It tells us that many years ago a merchant owed more money to a rascally money-lender than he could possibly pay back. The merchant also had a beautiful daughter whom the money-lender lusted after, with the result that he proposed a horrifying bargain to father and daughter. The bargain, however, was presented in a rather peculiar way, as if to suggest that the money-lender, though ruthless, was not such a bad fellow in his own way. Standing talking to the merchant and his girl on a pebble-strewn path, the money-lender proposed that Providence should decide the issue. He would put one black and one white pebble in a money-bag, and the girl herself could reach in and choose one. If she chose black, then she would become the money-lender's wife and the merchant's debts would be forgotten. If she chose white, she was free of his attentions and *still* the debts would be forgotten. Who could say fairer than that?

The cornered pair had to agree. When the money-lender stooped to gather up his pebbles, however, the worried young woman saw that he had taken not one black and one white but two black pebbles, and dropped them slyly into the bag. With a smile, he then asked her to choose.

What, asks de Bono, would we do, in this situation? He suggests that vertical thinking would concentrate on the choice, worrying about injustice, whether to denounce the rogue, to refuse to co-operate, or simply to sacrifice oneself for the good of one's parent. Lateral thinking, he then proposes, is quite radically different –

and the daughter used it to great effect. In effect she was as sly as the money-lender, using the same sleight-of-hand. She reached into the bag for a stone, fumbled as she drew it out, dropped it before anyone could see its colour, then blushed and said: 'How clumsy I am! But never mind, we can just look at the one that is left. Its colour will tell us which I chose.'

And the money-lender's evil ploy was foiled.

It is interesting and informative that de Bono chose as a lead-in to his book a folk-tale or an example cast in the form of folk wisdom. A great deal of folk wisdom – much of it now in cliché form – gains its power from the unitive quality of its material. There are riddles to be solved, Gordian knots to be cut, labyrinths to be escaped from using clever clues – the trickster can be on both sides, and guile succeeds over guile because it uses the magic of non-normal, non-linear and often 'mythic' styles of thinking. It is as often right-brained as it is left-brained, and it need come as no surprise that the laterality of de Bono's techniques has been compared with the 'lateralization' of the hemispheres of the brain. As Charles Hampden-Turner has it, in *Maps of the Mind* (1981):

> 'Lateral thinking . . . displays the characteristics attributed to the right hemisphere. It is timeless, diffuse, holistic, visuo-spatial, intuitive and simultaneous. Its aim is to synthesize new whole patternings and it scans intuitively over patterns and pieces searching for a simultaneous fit, regardless of their sequences of arrival.'

Few people in recent years have done as much to promote the active and explicit teaching of thinking as Edward de Bono. In 20 years of writing, lecturing and consulting he has advocated that instead of ignoring 'thinking skills' in education – or at best handling them obliquely through other subjects, hoping that somehow people will pick them up – we should, throughout the world, be packaging the kind of techniques that he has described in his various books so as to make future generations more competent than ourselves in appreciating the potential and also the limitations of thought. It is a subject, he argues convincingly, that is inherently as teachable as reading, writing and arithmetic.

To facilitate the improvement of the world's thoughts about thinking de Bono has set up on the island of Malta, his birthplace, an institution called SITO, the Supranational Independent Thinking

Organization. The *International Herald Tribune* of 24 July 1986 has described it as 'an intellectual Red Cross, functioning outside political, national and ideological frameworks', offering its creative services in attempts to resolve such perennial issues as sectarianism is Northern Ireland and racism in South Africa. It will also initiate studies in areas like famine, unemployment, and nuclear energy, sometimes providing confidential reports, sometimes operating publicly.

'Several weeks ago,' wrote Joan Z. Shore, in the *Tribune* report, 'Dr de Bono conducted the first meeting of SITO, a week of daily discussions in Malta. About a dozen people attended, hand-picked by Dr de Bono. They included an economist from Chile, an Islamic scholar and educator from Malaysia, a West African lawyer from London, a Swedish industrialist and a maritime lawyer from New York. They were selected not for their particular expertise but their creative approach to thinking and problem-solving.'

The kind of innovative thinking that could arise out of a group like de Bono's SITO is hinted at in the following excerpt from Hampden-Turner, where he sums up the difference between vertical and lateral styles of thought:

> 'Vertical thinking is always controlled by a dominant idea [and] imposes a pre-fabricated technique upon reality. It is a self-maximizing, self-perpetuating system with, in social terms, much arrogance and rigidity of mind. An advanced industrial society with a pre-programmed, vertically thinking technostructure is potentially an ecological nightmare and a militaristic monster with its logical means of destruction firmly rooted in archaic value patterns. What intensifies this bias is that the achievements of lateral thinking can always be reconstructed by philosophers and historians of science to look like vertical thinking.
>
> For thousands of years we heard gods commanding us with injunctions equivalent to . . . "Think of the pebble still in the bag". We would thank gods or daemons for the inspiration, and thank logic for moving us from premise to conclusion. When religion began to wane, the logical positivists and assorted Pope-bashers tried to persuade us that Logic had done it all, that Progress was a vertical line down which dispassionate scientists trod the stepping stones to truth . . . But this is a caricature of how the inquiring mind works, of the metaphors, the heuristic devices, the false steps to true conclusions, the conceptual leaps and lucky breaks.'

Hampden-Turner also offers some sterling advice to the super-enthusiast. He says that those who go overboard into lateral thinking and dabble with it to their heart's content are in much the same condition as those who ardently remain fixated to linearity: 'Lateral and vertical, right hemisphere and left, must work together.'

The same warning applies to the idea of unitive thinking. Many people have at various times gone overboard in the quest for transcendental awareness, Cosmic Consciousness or some other avatar of the unitive idea. It is not enough to pronounce that 'I am at one with the cosmos', just as both well-worked logic and well-applied lateralism are not available without effort and understanding. All are powerful interrelated tools like knives; when properly sharpened and ready for use they can also cut the careless user. No one of the three is a substitute for any of the others, applied properly in its place.

Does this mean, then, that 'unitive thinking' is different in kind from 'linear' and 'lateral thinking'? Well, in typically 'evasive' unitive style one has to say 'Yes' *and* 'No' – it is and it isn't; it all depends. In the broadest possible sense of the term, unitiveness includes the linearity favoured by the left hemisphere and the laterality made available by the right hemisphere. In that same sense, as I suggested in Chapter 5, it includes instinct, emotion and intuition as well as intellectuality because we have and need all of these in order to operate as full humans. It is integrative and employs them all separately or together as the need arises. In a narrower sense, however, unitive thinking is distinct from instinct, emotion, intuition, linearity and laterality because it depends upon an acquired attitude to existence itself. It is, let us be frank, the attitude traditionally referred to as 'transcendental' and understood by yogis, Sufis, Zen Masters and other applied mystics as lying beyond language and symbolism. As such, it is the fourth of the four perceptions of Nyaya: not sense perception, although it uses it, not mental perception, though it uses that too, not consciousness of self, although that is brought in as well, but 'yogic intuition'.

The Greek source of the word 'mystic' relates both to initiation into a well-kept secret and to keeping the lips closed in silence – either in order to keep that secret or because silence is the essential nature of the experience that mystics have traditionally sought. In India, the *muni* is a sage who has taken a vow of silence – or, more fully, one who has understood the nature of the silence that lies beyond all words. Both conceptions, Greek and Hindu, serve as a reminder that language is a strictly limited tool – as are logic and lateral thinking. Unitive thinking as I am describing it in this book is also a strictly limited tool (especially as regards its immediate applications via various specific techniques and diagrams). It is not, however, a limited tool if and when it refers to a degree of awareness that is wordless and timeless.

It is at points like this that many pragmatic people who are deeply committed to logic and 'realism' (and who may well also be endowed with lateral skills) shrug and give up – employing, as part of the process, a despairing upward turning of the eyes. It can also be a point at which many poetic and romantic people (deeply committed to lateralism and emotional intuition) rhapsodize about the Inner Light and the Way of the Masters. These are both common but antithetical responses, and neither helps very much in any discussion of what Sisir Kumar Ghose at Santiniketan in India has referred to as a 'more sober' and 'maturer' approach to the subject of mystical experience (in his intriguing discussion of the subject in the *Encyclopaedia Britannica*, 15th edition). Like Aurobindo and Teilhard de Chardin, Ghose believes that the mystical outlook has its place in human evolutionary development, and sums it up as follows:

> There is obviously something nonmental, alogical, paradoxical, and unpredictable about the mystical phenomenon, but it is not, therefore, irrational or antirational or "religion without thought". Rather, as Zen masters say, it is knowledge of the most adequate kind, only it cannot be expressed in words. If there is a mystery about mystical experience, it is something it shares with life and consciousness. Mysticism, a form of living in depth, indicates that man, a meeting ground of various levels of reality, is more than one-dimensional . . . Though mysticism may be associated with religion, it need not be. The mystic often represents a type that the religious institution does not and cannot produce and does not know what to do with if and when one appears.'

Everyday thinking – whatever forms it may take, whether vertical or lateral – depends very much on language and pictorial symbolism. As we have seen in the preceding chapters, the unitive approach to life can use language and pictorial symbolism to great effect, in the process employing logic on the one hand and parable on the other. Since, however, the essential nature of the unitive lies beyond language and depiction, it is curiously and dynamically linked with *potentiality* rather than actuality, with *fluidity* rather than fixity. This is why anyone who talks or writes about it is constrained to deal in options and shapes, shifting the scenery swiftly in order to break a picture and replace it with another – as if hoping that the 'real' picture can be seen through the cracks between the earlier and the later images. But there we go again into the language of metaphor. But try it with another metaphor still: Edward de Bono calls such techniques 'insight switch-over' – and they work.

Although language ultimately fails us, it is remarkable how far it can be made to stretch. De Bono has been particularly effective in testing the elasticity of both language and the mind by inventing a new mini-word to accompany YES and NO. That word is *PO*, which I take to be an abbreviation of POtential and POssible. It is, he says in *PO: Beyond YES and NO* (1972), 'a magic word' that 'will do all you want it to do if you believe in it' and 'as with all magic, the more you believe the better it works'. It is a word, he adds, that though magical comes from science and mathematics, and although it has been created by a specialist in thinking is equally attractive to hippies and the heads of big business corporations, to artists and computer enthusiasts. He is strongly assertive both about it and about us:

> The world is divided into two sorts of people: the PO people and the NOPO people. Only they do not know it yet. You yourself will not know whether you are a PO person or a NOPO person until you have finished reading this book. At the end you will have a very clear idea, because you will either understand PO or hate it. You will also be able to look around at your friends, your family, your boss, the people you work with, your politicians, and any other people in your life and decide whether they are PO people or NOPO people.'

De Bono relates a taste for PO to creatively inclined individuals like poets, designers and younger people with an eye to the future, while those who dislike or resist it are typically politicians and philosophers, lawyers and literary critics, and those traditional academics who enjoy building the elegant edifices of yesterday's thought. There is certainly something exciting and challenging about PO, as can be seen from the following, where PO is used as an interjection:

> 'Young people today have no backbone, no discipline. What they need is a spell of military service.'
> 'PO!'
> 'All the troubles of the modern world are due to the loosening of moral standards.'
> 'PO!'

There is something strikingly Zen-like here, as the monosyllable explodes in contradiction, inviting one to escape from a particular point of view. It can certainly be lateral and innovative, but in the way in which it operates it may not always be *unitive*. Zen masters offer their powerful blows to the ego, in the main, only to those who have submitted to their regimens, or those who may thoroughly deserve a sharp rejoinder. Direct assault on the minds of the unenlightened (or the supposedly unenlightened), however, is a disunitive rather than a unitive approach, and needs to be handled with great care. In the same way, the first option of the split circle is a powerful but limited one, and in presenting PO de Bono opts for it rather than something less contentious and more persuasive: 'The world is divided into two sorts of people, the PO people and the NOPO people.' There may well be some truth in that, from a certain viewpoint, but it is equally likely that, as regards PO, people will string themselves out along a continuum of responses, being more PO or less PO wherever they go (after all, it does depend . . .).

And there is always the risk of that very arrogance which de Bono and other commentators feel is detrimental to human progress. If I am a PO person and you are not, then my situation is better than yours, I am among the Elect and Enlightened, and you are not. My analogue, at the end of the day, becomes better than your analogue, and we are divided the one from the other once more. PO!

Follow-up to Chapter 9

● Here are two quotations from Tony Buzan's *Use Your Head* (1984):

'For the last few hundred years it has been popularly thought that man's mind worked in a linear or list-like manner. This belief was held primarily because of the increasing reliance on our two main methods of communication, speech and print.'

'The brain's non-linear character is . . . confirmed by recent biochemical physiological and psychological research. Each area of research is discovering that the organism is not only non-linear but is so complex and interlinked as to defy any final description.'

○ How do you respond to the idea that the output of a non-linear mind/brain is poured into linear presentation?

○ Is it possible that the Urbanians' love of linearity – and especially squares – could come to an end? If it did, what might replace it?

○ What is the unitive implication of Buzan's remarks, especially in his final comments?

● It is often said that the ancient Greeks' early interest in logic arose out of the study of geometry, especially in ancient Egypt. Urbanian interest in squares might well have come from the same source, and yet all sorts of non-linear, other-than-logical points have been made in this book by drawing upon geometrical devices. What conclusion might one draw about this surprising interest in neat shapes and structures?

● Context and reference are always important in any kind of thinking; even in the most decontextualized kinds of unitive thinking some link with the familiar is essential, at least as a starting-point. Here is a famous statement by one of the first great manufacturers and distributors of the automobile, Henry Ford:

History is bunk.

It has no context, and yet it is generally taken to mean something. What do you suppose that it means?

● In a letter to *The Observer* (3 August 1986), Ronald Frenburgh wrote: 'In the course of an assignment for the *Toronto Star* I spent a morning with Mr [Henry] Ford in 1935. He was easy to talk to and I asked him if he had in fact said that "history is bunk". "Yes," he replied, "and I'll tell you why I said it. As a young man I was very interested in how people lived in earlier times; how they got from place to place, lighted their homes, cooked their meals and so on. So I went to the history books. Well, I could find out all about the kings and presidents; but I could learn nothing of their everyday lives. So I decided that history is bunk."'

Was this your interpretation of the phrase? What benefit do we gain from the Frenburgh letter? What is its unitive value?

● The following quotation is from Claude M. Bristol, *The Magic of Believing* (1948):

'After studying the various mystical religions and different teachings and systems of mind-stuff, one is impressed with the fact that they all have the same basic *modus operandi*, and that is through repetition – the repeating of certain mantras, words, formulas, or just plain mumbo-jumbo.'

Can you see any value in such repetition, even of mumbo-jumbo?

● Here is what Ernest Wood says about the mystical syllable OM in Hinduism, in *Yoga* (1959):

'First, it must be clearly stated that the *mantras* used in yoga (many yogis do not use them) are for the purpose of proceeding towards the infinite, not for material gain . . . Therefore *Om* is recited for upward-going, and that is why its three parts, which are the letters a, u, and m, are respectively representatives of body, soul, and spirit.'

Compare both this and Bristol's remarks with the following from Edward de Bono's *PO: Beyond YES and NO*:

'The Hindu chant "Om", through constant repetition, comes to act as a conditioning signal to bring about a feeling of detachment. In the same way you could condition yourself to react to PO as a tranquillizing signal for use in tense or anxious situations.'

Does this make PO a mantra?

● Below is a poem entitled 'My Universe is True':

MY universe is true, and
YOURS is false, because
I am a fortunate true believer, and
YOU are an infidel –

Heathenish
Pagan
A Kaffir
Not saved by the blood, or the thread, or the book, or the
    foreskin
Unconfirmed
Unchosen
Inelect
Out in the dark with wrong ideas –
Well-meaning, no doubt, but
NOT like me
(though I never boast or vaunt myself)
YOU are not saved,
Not secure or born again, like
ME
Not resurrected into truth
With the Right People
The Chosen People
My People
MINE.

10

Open Circles

'When you are deeply asleep,' writes Colin Wilson, 'you have no consciousness. When you are very tired, your consciousness is like a dim light that hardly illuminates anything. When you are wide awake and excited, consciousness seems to increase in sheer candle-power. Its purpose is to illuminate reality, to reach out into its recesses, and thus enable us to act upon it and transform it. It is obvious that our basic aim should be to increase its candle-power. When it is low, reality becomes "unreal"; as it becomes stronger, reality becomes "realler": Faculty X.'

In 1971, in his book *The Occult*, Colin Wilson presented this 'Faculty X' as a quality that we have used in the past, can use now, and could use even more effectively in the future. It is the common denominator of all paranormal phenomena, much as electricity is the shared force behind modern lighting and the animation of radios, television and many other appliances. The metaphor that he uses to discuss both this quality and the nature of consciousness is also linked to electricity: light, candle-power, illumination. The greater the illumination, the greater the consciousness.

'What are you then?' a brahmin priest asked Gautama Siddhartha some 2,500 years ago. 'Are you a god, a demi-god, some spirit or an ordinary man?'

'None of these,' said the Buddha. 'I am awake.'

The idea of 'unitive thinking' as I have outlined it in the preceding chapters is obviously linked with such matters as the Buddha's enlightenment and Wilson's Faculty X, although I have deliberately kept the discussion away from altered states of consciousness, meditation, spiritual regimes, special supernormal powers, and the like. It has not been my aim to discuss the whole broad phenomenon of mysticism and the paranormal, but rather to extract from it a part of its ideology – a part of the idea system that animates it. The end-product is a mental partner, as it were, to those books that have extracted physical exercises from the complex of yoga. Just as those books have as their aim the improvement and greater vigour of the body, so this book has as its focus of interest the improvement and greater vigour of the mind. But in addition, just as those books may fail to deliver on their own such a physical improvement, so this book can easily fail to provide on its own the increase in mental vigour – the greater degree of candle-power or awakeness – that many of us are interested in.

To illustrate this we can go back to the parable of the sower, which is one of the great archetypal pictures of the relationship between teacher and taught – whatever is being taught and whoever the learner may be. The seeds are scattered, in this botanical metaphor, and fall all over the place. Some fall on the footpath, where they are simply squashed lifeless under the feet of many travellers with other things on their minds. Some fall on rocky ground, hard unyielding places where there is no soil at all. Some fall among thistles and other plants that are already well established, and fail to find space and nourishment in which to put down strong roots and rise up to meet the sun and the rain. And some fall on good, open soil, where they flourish.

This parable both tells the statistical truth about messages of any kind and also – marvellously – protects the ego of the messenger, the sower. After all, if you scatter your seeds, there are four outcomes; accept this, be prepared for all four, and you have insured yourself against the world. It also operates a container model, in which the seed-message ends up in four distinct and separate category-places: the footpath box, the rocky-ground box, the thistle box, and the good-soil box. Even if you change it to a continuum model, then the fate of the seeds is along a line from rejection at one end to acceptance at the other, with all sorts of intermediate responses in between, including what for me is a most intriguing additional element: that some people will take the seeds and hybridize the resulting plants with others of their own, and create further and different-yet-similar plants. One reason for this is that we all bring our own backgrounds to reading and listening, and all impose our own intepretations upon what we read and hear. Discuss this book with a friend who has also read it, and this basic and invaluable 'truth' will become clear. Discuss it with more people still, and the whole gamut of footpath responses, rocky-ground responses, thistle responses, good-soil responses, groupie responses, hybridizing responses and other *wholly unforeseeable* responses will emerge.

It is not unusual in books that are essentially manuals of one kind or another to list in the final chapter a résumé of points relating to earlier chapters, drawing them together tidily and usefully into a conclusion that serves as an overview of the subject (often linking up with something in the introduction or the first chapter, so that the line of text with its container-chapters becomes an aesthetically pleasing circle). Let's not do that, however. Rather than say what *I* think has been unfolding, I will simply list instead certain main points of each chapter so that you can examine your own responses to them. These are also incidentally useful as mnemonic devices – even as a kind of index of what has been going on. Like many mnemonic devices these depend for effect upon their very 'bizarreness'; one may remember better what is linked to them than if they were résumés of a more conventional kind (see box).

The lists for each chapter are as linear as the ordering of the chapters themselves. If, however, there is a tight logical structure to the 'argument' running through the chapters it is certainly not detectable in the lists, which are a series of isolated and (to the casual eye) quirky phrases. This itself is a significant point, because it creates a kind of separation among the people of the world, not unlike de Bono's PO and NOPO people. In terms of these lists there *are* only two kinds of people in the world: those for whom the lists make some sort of sense (the people who have read the book) and those for whom the lists make little or no sense (the people who haven't read the book, either because they have never encountered it, because they have encountered it and decided not to bother with it, or have begun it and given up before the lists could begin to make sense).

A mnemonic résumé

Chapter 1. Split Circles
the superthriller and the South Korean flag
Sean Connery: yinning and yanging around
sunlight and shadow on a hill
Yin and/or Yang: the three options
Kipling's impostors
clockwise or counter-clockwise

Chapter 2. Pregnant Triangles
Yajnavalkya and the half-fragments
Shiva and Shakti in love
Star Hexagons and Shri Yantras
view from a rear window
the Mouth of Time
Maya
containers and continuums
a Glasgow love story
Protestant and Catholic Jews

Chapter 3. Frames and Fables
the kluuls from Arcturus
Zerubavel and the Seven-day Circle
the chronobiologists
the yoga headstand
the Great Egg Shell of Hermopolis
Maya and Brahman: cutting up the seamless robe

Chapter 4. Parabolas
Cube meets Globe
the Parable of the Sower
Animal Farm
the world of 'as if'
the *Bhagavad-Gita* and the battlefield of life
Plato's Cave
the enlightenment of St Thomas Aquinas
'My analogue is better than your analogue!'
world epics

Chapter 5. Compartments of the Brain
brain or brains?
crocodile, horse and mirror twins
Jekyll and Hyde, Beauty and the Beast
kluul sheaths and human bodies
hard reality, soft reality
clichés with power
Homunculus

Chapter 6. Ladders of the Mind
Urbanian squares
Bokanovskify!
brahmins, kshatriyas and caste
Buddha and the Noble Eight-Fold Path
Patanjali's Eight-Limb Yoga
Darwin's ladder of life
the Piaget–Koplowitz rungs of awareness
the Maslow ladder of needs
Zen ladders with no rungs

Chapter 7. Centres of Self
Jamlu's people
Toynbee's world
closed against open
incest
centricity
eccentricity

Chapter 8. The Scale of Things
Flat-earthists in an infinite universe
macrocosm, microcosm and 'mesocosm'
rippling rocks
Gensha and the swallow
the Tao of physics
Yin of materialism, Yang of spiritualism
cosmologists, every one
turtles all the way down

The result is a small in-group (the readers) and a vast out-group (the rest of humanity). If the in-group were cohesive enough, and enthusiastic enough, then one member might nudge another at a cocktail party, wink, and say, 'Aha, Jamlu's people', or, 'They're really stuck with the rear-view window, aren't they?' The cosiness – even the arrogance – of in-group membership might arise, with the odd result that a new bunch of Jamlu's people could emerge, fixated on one particular vision labelled 'unitive thinking'.

This possibility may serve to explain the relative exclusiveness of unitive thinkers in the past – or at least go some way towards accounting for this often unattractive facet of the subject. In-groups often work because of their secret codes and signs. Such codes and signs might exist in order to emphasize a secret togetherness and a Gnostic doctrine, might simply arise because they are the necessary symbolism and language of the group, or might be a mixture of both. Medical jargon is a case in point, where sometimes the high-sounding Greek polysyllables serve simply to blind the outsider (usually the patient) but as often are simply the traditional vocabulary of a complex craft; it is also often hard to decide where the one stops and the other begins, and medical people may be the least able to talk about the matter. There is a pride in being an in-grouper, saying with a knowing sigh, 'Ah yes, the Kauderwelsch Gambit – now let's see if she uses the Quatsch Manoeuvre!' One belongs; one is in the know.

But while recognizing that this element is important, there is also the matter of appropriateness and mnemonics. Much of unitive thinking dates from pre-literate times, circulated among people who did not record information in books. As a result what they said has had to be both compact and memorable, and memory often works better with curious pegs to hang things on, odd parables to explain the inexplicable, and sharp devices to focus the attention. Even in our time, when books are easily available and are (for the moment) the principal means through which information and ideas are disseminated, mnemonic tricks and an appropriate 'jargon' are still useful – otherwise, the material cannot so easily pass from the page (where it is inert) to the mind (where it can join in the general ferment of experience).

But what about the cocktail party and the knowing whisper about Jamlu's people? What about the pride of the Gnostic?

It is at this point that we can no longer separate unitiveness from the broad matrix to which it belongs. In the introduction to this book I said that unitive thinking isn't new. That is so, but at the same time 'unitive thinking' as I have presented it here *is* new, because it has never, to my knowledge, been separated out from the traditions of mysticism in this way, and certainly has not been shaped in the particular container-like ways that I have chosen to use. The background unitive thinking of human history could be shaped in an infinite range of such containers, but the foreground unitive thinking – mine, the form of this book – has only one shape, necessarily. That is both good and bad. It is good, because it leads to the subject being aired; it is bad because by having taken on *this* shape it may close off the possibility of other equally interesting shapes.

The matrix to which unitive thinking broadly belongs appears to have begun in the formulations (magical, religious, mystical, mythological, philosophical, etc., as we refer to them nowadays) of all kinds of shamans, priests, yogis and ascetics since people first began to speculate about their existence and look for tools to give them power over nature. It finds expression both in oral 'folk-wisdom' (all sorts of adages and aphorisms, proverbs and clichés) as well as in oral-cum-literary 'scriptures', where again magic, superstition, the supernatural, religion, philosophy, law and social order all blend together. There may have been something of a free-for-all long ago – nobody knows – but all the records that survive suggest that human societies around the world have tended to regulate the body of lore in which unitive thinking has been embedded through the agency of priesthoods, monastic orders, hermit communities, secret societies and the like. These might range from the deeply orthodox, strictly controlling the mystical adventures of their members, to a variety of charismatics and others whose activities attracted the misgivings and sometimes the persecution of orthodoxy – although such rebels could well in due course become the basis for new orthodoxies.

I have presented the unitive approach to life as a series of overlapping techniques and conceptions. These might be in the form of traditional symbolism (the Yin–Yang circle of ancient China, the Shiva–Shakti triangles of ancient India), in the form of parables (ancient parables like the New Testament Sower of Seeds; new parables like *Animal Farm*, Urbania, or the kluuls from Arcturus), or extrapolated from such devices in the form of recognizable 'principles' such as multiple options, containers and continuums, reversal and inversion, analogic, juxtaposition of things usually never juxtaposed, paradoxes, and so forth. There is no obviously 'right' way of ordering such things, and I have therefore refrained from ordering them in anything other than a useful sequence for my own purposes.

Despite the inevitable tendency towards in-groupiness wherever a set of techniques is offered and taken up, the curious thing about the whole background of unitive thinking is the openness of the 'secret'. To apply another cliché, which is also a paradox, the secret is that *there is no secret*. To apply a parable, it is like the man who left his home to find a fabled treasure, and who, after much wandering, at last obtained a map locating the hoard. He followed the map, right back to his own home, where he dug under his own chair, and found the treasure.

Unitive thinking belongs in a matrix of experience from which, ultimately, it cannot be separated out and served up as a dish on its own. Proof of this is provided in the ladders of the Buddha and Patanjali, in the religious background to Christ's parables, and in the essentially 'spiritual' aspects of Yin–Yang and the symbols of

Shiva and Shakti. It is quite possible that someone with criminal or dishonest aims in life could apply on an *ad hoc* basis various of the techniques that I have been looking at. Certainly the ancient stories of yoga in India abound with demons wringing boons from the very gods through the intensity and sincerity of their ascetic practices. Most of the unitive systems of the world, however, have a strong ethical element to them, an element that has a chicken-and-egg quality about it. Are ethical principles attached to the unitive way because they are necessary to restrain the ego of the practitioner, or is the unitive path such that it promotes an ethical style of life?

This question can only be posed because I have artificially, as it were, separated out unitive thinking from the rest of the matrix of mysticism. In religious contexts any kind of spiritual adventuring is usually surrounded by caveats and commandments of various kinds, but it also seems likely that in systems like yoga, Sufism and Zen people can hardly travel along the transcendental path without acquiring certain attitudes and kinds of behaviour that can only be described as ethical: refraining from harsh criticism of others as much as possible (but at times engaging in it when it is judged necessary), refraining from lies, theft and possessiveness (but not necessarily always recommending total honesty and directness, or universal poverty), refraining from injuring or killing any living thing (but making exceptions on occasion, either for themselves in special circumstances, or certain 'right' occupations, such as the honourable soldier). Individuals and groups vary in their approach to such matters as integrity, individual and society, sexuality and celibacy, pacifism, vegetarianism, and so forth, but by and large the rule is the Golden Rule. It seems very likely that anyone with anything resembling a unitive outlook on life endorses – for logical as well as emotional, for practical as well as mystical reasons – the principle that you do to others what you would have them do to you.

And one faces life with as much courage and compassion as can be drawn from within oneself.

In 1974, Robert M. Pirsig brought out a book with the title *Zen and the Art of Motorcyle Maintenance*, adding in the author's note that it was based on real experience, but 'should in no way be associated with that great body of factual information relating to orthodox Zen Buddhist practice' and is 'not very factual on motorcycles, either'. All of which seems to me to have the right twist to it, like the ineffable smile on the faces of both the Cheshire Cat and the Buddha. In his book, Pirsig has something to say that serves admirably to bring this particular work to a close, allying thought with both attitude and behaviour:

> 'I like the word "gumption", because it's so homely and so forlorn and so out of style it looks as if it needs a friend and isn't likely to reject anyone who comes along. It's an old Scottish word, once used a lot by pioneers, but which, like "kin", seems to have all but dropped out of use. I like it also because it describes exactly what happens to someone who connects with Quality. He gets filled with gumption. The Greeks called it *enthousiasmos*, the root of "enthusiasm", which means literally "filled with *theos*," or God, or Quality. See how that fits?
>
> 'A person filled with gumption doesn't sit around dissipating and stewing about things. He's at the front of the train of his own awareness, watching to see what's up the track and meeting it when it comes. That's gumption . . .
>
> 'The gumption-filling process occurs when one is quiet long enough to see and hear and feel the real universe, not just one's own stale opinions about it. But it's nothing exotic. That's why I like the word . . . If you're going to repair a motorcycle, an adequate supply of gumption is the first and most important tool.'

Amen to that.

Follow-up to Chapter 10

● Compare these passages. The writers appear to be talking about the same thing, but how do their tones and their metaphors differ, and what does the difference tell us?

> The trouble is *the narrowness of consciousness*. It is as if you tried to see a panoramic scene through cracks in a high fence, but were never allowed to look *over* the fence and see it as a whole. And the narrowness lulls us into a state of permanent drowsiness, like being half-anaesthetised, so that we never attempt to stretch our powers to their limits. With the consequence that we never discover their limits.' (Colin Wilson, *The Occult*, 1971)

> 'So be assured, dear earthling, that you are a parcel of all mankind, of all life, of all matter, of all mind, of all spirit in the Universe. Even though the Mystery includes a veil to hide its awesome Glory from

our feeble understanding, console yourself that your skin and senses are really less the boundary they always seemed than a bridge joining you to the world. And, as truly, the Universe is more than the pattern of matter we sense, for it is literally the greater aspect of one's own self. With profound confidence, then, and lovingly, may we pray: "Thy will be done, O Universe!"'
(Guy Murchie, *The Seven Mysteries of Life*, 1978)

● There have been several variant uses of the basic Yin–Yang circle in this book. The diagram shows another. You may or may not have met it before. If you have, you are a member of the in-group, and its significance is immediate. If you have not, then you may be able to make little sense of it, apart from the basic sense. When ready, have a look at the symbol's significance, at the foot of the page.

● In *Mysticism and the New Physics* (1980), Michael Talbot observes: 'There is something maddening about answers to metaphysical questions. Anyone who has ever puzzled over a Zen proverb must know this frustration. Time and again the "answer" seems to be there, but one cannot find it. It is as if it is lost in semantic hocus-pocus.'
How do you feel about that comment?

Talbot goes on: 'The wisdom of the ancient teachings hides behind the cosmically ambiguous, and all that saves us from throwing up our hands is the promise that the "answer" *is* there, it simply cannot be put into words.'

The Yin–Yang with AA is the symbol of the Anti-Apartheid Movement, whose headquarters in 1986 were at 13 Mandela Street, London NW1, England.

How do you feel about *that* comment?

● Alvin Toffler is the leading futurist of our time. In 1970 he published *Future Shock* and in 1980 *The Third Wave*. The core thesis of both books is that the human race is dividing – or has divided – into three groups:

1 *yesterday's people*: a first wave of humanity still bonded to the farming revolution of the New Stone Age
2 *today's people*: a second wave of humanity still bonded to the ideas and activities of the Industrial Revolution
3 *tomorrow's people*: a third wave of humanity belonging to a new 'worldwide superindustrial society now in the throes of its birth'.

Of his second book he says: 'The Third Wave is for those who think the human story, far from ending, has only just begun.'

Of Toffler's views, Edward de Bono says: 'We have been given a taste of the future and we do not like it, because we cannot see how we are going to cope with it. Books like Alvin Toffler's *Future Shock* have spelled out the future in all its difficulty. But complaining about the future will not stop it. The more change there is, the more chaos there will be, since chaos is caused by different rates of change in different parts of the system . . . We came to the end of an intellectual era some years ago. This was the end of the era that had started so long ago with the ancient Greek philosophers. The end of the era was not recognized in any formal way, because the traditional intellectuals whose business it is to note such changes are themselves too much part of the old era to notice them.' (*PO: Beyond YES and NO*)

And Colin Wilson adds, from *The Occult*: 'Faculty X is not a "sixth sense", but an ordinary potentiality of consciousness. And it should be clear from what I have written above that it is the key not only to so-called occult experience, but to the whole future evolution of the human race . . . Man's future lies in the cultivation of Faculty X.'

Does it? Should it? And *have* we seen the future?

● Try these:

'A leaderless but powerful network is working to bring about radical change in the United States. Its members have broken with key elements of Western thought, and they may even have broken continuity with history. This network is the Aquarian Conspiracy. It is a conspiracy without a political doctrine. Without a manifesto. With conspirators who seek power only to disperse it, and whose strategies are pragmatic, even scientific, but whose perspective sounds so mystical that they hesitate to discuss it . . . Broader than reform, deeper than revolution, this benign conspiracy for a new human agenda has triggered the most rapid cultural realignment in history. The great shuddering, irrevocable shift overtaking us is not a new political, religious, or philosophical system. It is a new mind – the ascendance of a startling worldview that gathers into its framework breakthrough science and insights from earliest recorded thought.' (Marilyn Ferguson, 1980, *The Aquarian Conspiracy*)

'The British people are moving in the right direction faster than the rest of the world – and against the tide of British politics, left and right. Therefore, 20 years on, Britain could be a winner in a post-industrial world, just as it led in the first industrial revolution. That awesomely optimistic verdict, with evidence to back it, comes in a huge and so far unpublished study made for the National Economic Development Office by Taylor Nelson Monitor. Stripped of its social-science jargon, the report's message is that Britain already has more of the New People than any other nation, bar the Netherlands . . . Already, the report shows, more than a third of the UK population rejects the rat-race conformity of the old industrial era. Ironically, it is today's peak nations – Japan, the United States, West Germany – which cling most solidly to these dying disciplines.' (Peter Large, 'Britain's New People are top of the world', The *Guardian*, 7 February 1986)

How do you feel about these quotes (a) if you are American, (b) if you are British, (c) if you are Dutch, (d) if you are anything else, (e) if you are a unitive thinker?

Index